WILD ANIMALS IN NEW ZEALAND

Whitetail deer buck (antlers not fully grown). Lower Dart Valley, Otago.

WILD ANIMALS IN NEW ZEALAND

Compiled under the direction of
A. L. POOLE
Director-General of Forests

Photographs by
J. H. JOHNS, ARPS
New Zealand Forest Service

A. H. & A. W. REED

WELLINGTON   AUCKLAND   SYDNEY   LONDON

First published 1969
Second impression 1971
Second edition 1973

A. H. & A. W. REED LTD
182 Wakefield Street, Wellington
51 Whiting Street, Artarmon, Sydney
11 Southampton Row, London WC1B 5HA
also
29 Dacre Street, Auckland
165 Cashel Street, Christchurch

ISBN 0 589 00411 5

Library of Congress Catalogue No. 76-597144

Printed and bound by Kyodo Printing Company Limited, Tokyo, Japan

CONTENTS

CONTRIBUTORS

J. E. C. Flux is a member of the Animal Ecology Division, Department of Scientific and Industrial Research; A. H. C. Christie, L. H. Harris, J. T. Holloway, P. C. Logan, K. H. Miers, and L. T. Pracy are officers of the New Zealand Forest Service.

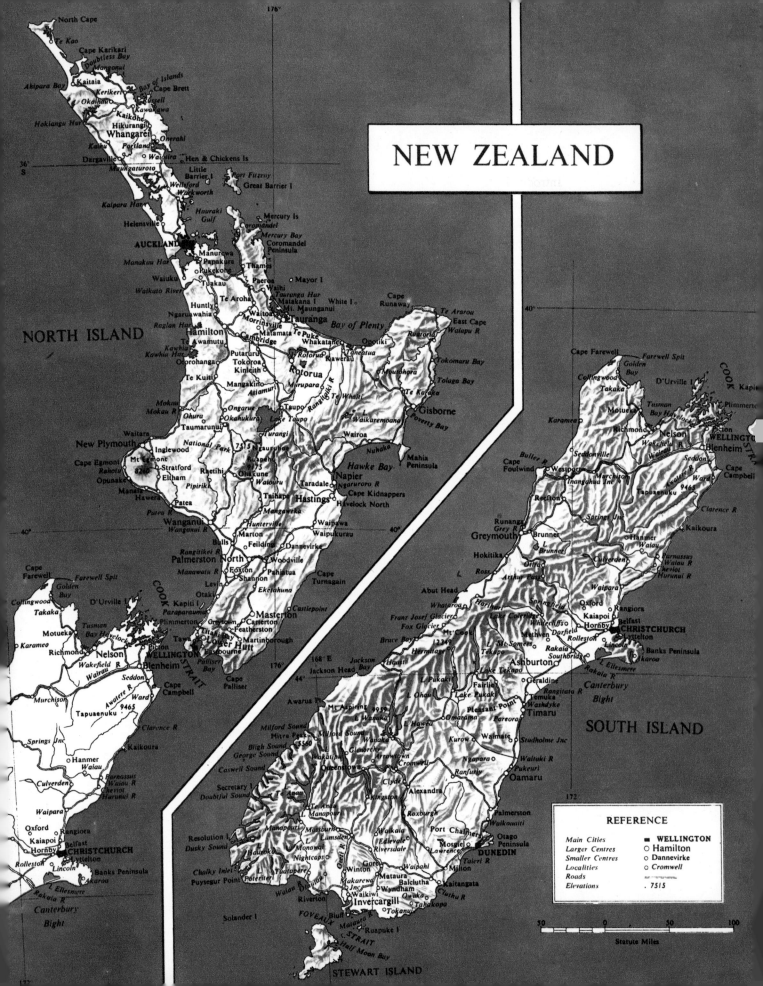

NEW ZEALAND

ILLUSTRATIONS

COLOUR PLATES

MAPS & DIAGRAMS

BLACK & WHITE PLATES

7

The photographs on pages 140 and 141 are by J. A. Mackintosh, Murihiku Game Farm, Southland; those on pages 134 and 135 are by T. Porter, Lake Coleridge; that on page 95 is by G. Field; and that on page 138 by National Publicity Studios. All others are by J. H. Johns, New Zealand Forest Service.

The maps showing distribution of game animals were prepared by Joyce Neil, New Zealand Forest Service, from Department of Lands and Survey base maps.

The drawings of antlers are based on diagrams prepared by National Publicity Studios.

8

INTRODUCTION

ALMOST ALL the wild animals that are common in New Zealand or that have been numerous were brought here, liberated, protected for a time, and encouraged to spread and increase. Over fifty species of animals (excluding domestic ones) were introduced, and thirty-five of them have become acclimatised.

Acclimatisation activity was sanctioned by early legislation, the intention of Acts passed in 1861 being to ". . . encourage the importation of . . . animals and birds not native to New Zealand which would contribute to the pleasure and profit of the inhabitants when they became acclimatised and were spread over the country in sufficient numbers". Not until 1895 was the consent of the Government needed to introduce any animal or bird.

The enthusiasm for the liberation of animals, especially those that would provide meat, began with Captain Cook, who on his first voyage in 1769 had noticed the absence of mammals. Therefore on his second voyage in 1773 he put pigs, goats, and sheep ashore in the Marlborough Sounds. The sheep very soon died, as a result, Cook thought, of eating a poisonous plant (very likely tutu), though the animals were in poor condition after the long voyage from the Cape of Good Hope.

Between the time of Cook's visits and the beginning of organised settlement by Europeans, sealers, whalers, and a few general traders set up shore bases and kept animals. Some may have been liberated and others are sure to have escaped from captivity. During this period and even much later there were plenty of opportunities for rats and mice to come ashore from ships.

As European settlement proceeded and domestic food-producing animals became well established interest turned to animals that could provide sport or furs. Little consideration seems to have been given to the implications of freeing animals to graze and browse at will on vegetation that had developed free of this pressure. An environment that greatly favoured free-ranging herbivorous animals was not well endowed to withstand their harmful effects. Nor were the adverse effects discerned as readily or as soon as was success in establishing the introduced animals. Nevertheless, from the beginning of this century uneasiness developed at the increase and spread of introduced animals.

Elaborate measures have been taken to eliminate rabbits or to greatly reduce their numbers, but such far-reaching schemes are unlikely to be practicable or necessary for other wild animals. The policy of the Forest Service is to reduce the numbers of wild animals to levels dictated by correct land use. Therefore outside those areas where organised control is imperative to reduce severe damage to vegetation there is ample opportunity for sport. Indeed this is an aspect of the multiple use of forest land which it is the policy to adopt as far as possible. The multiple-use concept means that all the resources are for use and that one requirement must not preclude other activities in the forest, including recreational activities such as hunting.

Not only is there still plenty of scope in New Zealand for the hunting of wild animals, but such activities are now recognised as a useful adjunct to organised animal control, which because of cost alone must be concentrated in high-priority areas where operations can be reasonably sure to produce worth-while results. In many parts of the country huts have been provided and access improved to encourage sportsmen to shoot in remote areas and so eventually to lower wild animal populations enough for forests to tolerate them.

A recent development has been the commercial hunting of deer for the export of venison: the value of the meat sold overseas, principally in West Germany and Holland, for the year ended June 1971 was NZ $4.7 million. Helicopters are being used to transport hunters and to collect carcasses from remote country. Commercial hunting will be payable only as long as deer are plentiful and inevitably areas will be worked out. The success of the industry has turned thoughts to the possibilities of farming deer to produce venison for export. A few deer farms have been started but have not been operating long enough to indicate how successful they are likely to be.

Of all the wild animals illustrated on the following pages only the bat, of which there are two species, and the Maori rat (kiore) are natives. Even the latter and the now extinct native dog (kuri) were brought from Polynesia in the thirteenth century or perhaps earlier. This book therefore presents, with the exceptions referred to, a somewhat unusual collection of pictures of animals in habitats they have occupied for less than 200 years.

INTRODUCED ANIMALS AND THE PROTECTION FORESTS
J. T. Holloway

THE QUESTION of whether the introduction of exotic game animals was a good or bad thing for New Zealand has been hotly debated for many years. Their introduction has indisputably resulted in the creation of a recreational and sporting asset very highly prized by many people, but it was evident even seventy-five years ago that serious damage would be done to the native forests.

The debate continues and is likely to continue indefinitely, because there is no simple answer. It is certain only that far-reaching changes in the composition and structure of the forests are under way; that the nature of these changes varies immensely from place to place and year to year in response to the complex interactions of a host of factors, including the effects of habitat modification on the animals themselves; and that the physical, economic, and other consequences of these events are equally variable. In brief, depending on which pair of spectacles we choose to wear and which piece of country we choose to look at, we can find evidence that can be used to support almost any argument that may be advanced.

The key fact, however, is that New Zealand is a mountainous land. The fertile, temperate lowlands where most of us live and work are of limited extent. Even where we do not live on the actual flood plains of the mountain-derived streams and rivers, our roads and railways cross these flood plains and most of the water for generation of electric power, for irrigation, and for industrial and domestic use comes from the mountains. As lowlanders, though we may never set foot in the mountains, we are singularly and inescapably dependent on proper management of mountain lands for our physical safety and economic well-being.

In practice, provided fire is adequately controlled and conditions have not deteriorated to the point where artificial land-rehabilitation measures must be adopted, proper management of the mountain lands largely becomes a matter of the proper control of the animals that have been introduced, because they present the greatest threat to the stability of catchments. The basic requirement is the maintenance at all times of a cover of vegetation dense enough to prevent excessive erosion. There will always be much erosion that cannot be prevented, but we cannot afford to let the rate increase to the point where the rivers can no longer cope with the quantities of erosion products reaching them.

This is the crux of the matter. In steep mountain country there is always much natural erosion. In the New Zealand mountains, for climatic and geological reasons, the normal rate can be very high by world standards. And in all such situations the balance between physical forces conducive to erosion and the restraining influence of vegetation is very fine and readily upset. Once introduced animals had found their way into the mountains it was inevitable that the balance would be upset, resulting in increased erosion and the filling up of stream channels. The only questions left open were how rapidly these changes would take place and how far they would proceed before new types of plant cover, better adjusted to the presence of animals, could evolve.

At first, little change was apparent. The virgin forests and associated subalpine scrublands and alpine grasslands had existed for thousands of years without being browsed by any animal. Accordingly there was an accumulation of food on which the animals could make only slow inroads. But this abundance (in combination with initial legal protection of wild animals, absence of predators, comparative freedom from disease and the mildness of winters) led to a rapid increase in animal numbers. Before long (approximately twenty-five to thirty years in the case of red deer in many beech forests) the accumulated food "capital" was exhausted. The animal population had now to live on the food "income", the annual growth of palatable plants surviving within their reach. This was the stage when damage to the forests was most conspicuous. Even dead leaves on the forest floor were sometimes licked up and eaten. Thereafter, animal population declined whether or not control operations were undertaken, but rarely to the point where forest capital could again accumulate on sites preferred by animals. Normally, a modest recovery of forest understoreys was evident where animals went only at times of peak population pressure and near-starvation.

Usually, of course, the effects of animals are much more complex than this. In any one valley, there are often many kinds of forest, valley and alpine grasslands, and scrubland. Two or more species of introduced animals are commonly present in any one area. Normal sequences of population growth and decline and normal patterns of animal distribution have frequently been irregularly distorted by hunting. But despite these complexities general trends remain much the same throughout the mountain forests as a whole. Only in a few special cases have trends been reversed; for example, in a few critically important river catchments where long-sustained, intensive control operations have been carried out, and in a few areas where, because of exceptionally ready access, private hunting has kept populations very low. Official control operations, private hunting, and commercial hunting for venison by helicopters have substantially reduced total animal numbers, but only the alpine grasslands have benefited much. The surviving animals are now concentrated in the upper forest zone, where conditions were already critical and control is much more difficult.

To emphasise these points, we can consider one situation of moderate complexity in somewhat greater detail. The mixed hardwood (rata-kamahi) forests of the Hokitika River catchment on the precipitous western flanks of the Southern Alps were originally very dense; so dense in fact and so wet under annual rainfall of 300-400 inches a year that conditions generally were unfavourable for red deer and opossums, despite an exceptional abundance of highly-preferred food plants. Above the timberline the subalpine scrublands were even denser. In many places they were, and are, virtually impenetrable. Initially, therefore, red deer could freely colonise only the alpine grasslands, thrusting in winter down relatively dry rocky ridges, open water-courses, and landslide scars into the forests.

Opossums could freely colonise only the rocky ridges, feeding very intensively on the scattered rata and kamahi trees growing there. These trees were soon killed, letting more sunlight and wind into the forest, thus improving the habitat for red deer. Meanwhile the deer had cut back the density of forest understoreys around their initial footholds, rendering additional areas suitable for colonisation by opossums.

By 1956-57, when these forests were first studied in detail, the alpine grasslands were moderately to severely depleted but the subalpine scrublands were still largely in virgin condition. In the forests, all conditions could be found from nearly untouched to advanced depletion. All or almost all undergrowth had been destroyed in stands near the timberline, on ridge crests, and in areas adjoining open watercourses. There had been no effective regeneration of forest on land-

slide scars for many years and mountain sides were liberally sprinkled with dead and dying rata and kamahi. But there were still many areas relatively untouched by animals and there was still an abundance of food.

Chamois had also entered the catchment, increasing grazing pressure on the alpine grasslands. There were indications that they would be capable of breaking into the subalpine scrublands, so far free of deer, and that the deer would then follow.

Thar (in 1956) were on the point of entering the catchment from the south. A natural decline in animal numbers was not in sight. Almost all tributary streams were showing signs of increasing bed loads and rising flood peaks.

Since 1956-57, intensive control operations in this catchment have markedly reduced the numbers of deer and chamois on the alpine grasslands and led to strong recovery of the grasslands. Many animal-induced erosion scars have healed or are healing. Similarly, there has been marked reduction in the number of opossums in the forests. There has been a substantial recovery of the forest canopy though, where many trees have been killed, more landslips must occur as tree roots, still holding the soil, decay and disintegrate. It is doubtful, however, whether deer numbers have yet been brought low enough in the forests. There has been little recovery of forest understoreys in severely depleted areas, especially near the timberline. Because of the amount of food available, any relaxation of control efforts would result in a rapid upsurge in animal numbers. No risks can be taken. Downstream flood hazards are acute.

In other catchments a degree of risk is possibly acceptable. The nature of the country is such that there is not the same high potential for acceleration of erosion and/or there may be a little downstream land liable to damage by flood. There are also forests where, though the forests are similar to those in the Hokitika River catchment, deer numbers could not build up rapidly to the same high levels because the alpine grasslands above the forests are largely composed of plants of very low palatability.

In effect, each and every area must be considered separately and treated on its merits. There are no universal rules. In no two river catchments do we face precisely the same combination of circumstances. In all cases, however, extreme caution must be exercised. Mistakes will be difficult and costly to correct, if indeed they can be rectified. Even if there is no im-
(continued on page 15)

The eastern flanks of the Southern Alps were once clothed with an almost continuous belt of forest, mostly mountain beech (*Nothofagus solandri* var. *cliffortioides*). Much of it has been burned, some before European times. What remains is valuable protection forest, which in many places is threatened by the depredations of sheep, deer, and other animals. When animals can be kept out of the forest it recovers vigorously. The prolific beech regeneration shown is in Craigieburn Forest, Canterbury.

The upper Travers Valley, Nelson, with a complete cover of beech forest up to the timber-line. The tops have been overgrazed by sheep, deer, and other wild animals. Although the forest at higher elevations has also been damaged to some extent, most of it is in good order. In a few places only does mountain-top erosion extend downhill.

RIGHT: Mt Fitzwilliam, at the Harper-Avoca confluence, eastern Southern Alps, has lost its original mantle of tussock grassland through overgrazing by sheep and to a lesser extent by deer. Animal browsing and the effects of frequent fires have also led to the destruction of the beech forest which occupied parts of it. When thus denuded the steep slopes are unstable. The startling erosion is an early phase of their readjustment to a stable angle.

14

mediate need for flood control, prevention of raising of the stream bed, or regulation of the useful water yield, we cannot yet see far enough ahead to be sure that such a need will never arise.

In the future, new types of forest, subalpine scrubland, and alpine grassland that can safely support game animal populations may evolve, but there are few signs of this happening yet, especially on critical high altitude sites. The conundrum is that, if we restore the vegetation to a semblance of its primitive condition by vigorous control of all introduced animals, there will never be an opportunity for new types of vegetation to evolve. But if we fail to do this, soil loss must continue to the point where over large areas it becomes impossible to maintain any effective plant cover.

Protection forests, including the subalpine scrublands and alpine grasslands, have values other than catchment protection and possible

(continued on page 17)

Forest in the Aorangi Mountains, southern Wairarapa. From the outside it looks normal but the interior has been severely depleted by cattle, goats, deer, pigs, and opossums. The forest floor has been denuded to such an extent (see photo opposite) that shingle slides have formed and slipping is taking place along streams. Control of animals is essential for recovery of the vegetation.

RIGHT: Interior of the forest shown above. The usual carpet of mosses, liverworts, ferns. etc. has disappeared; there is no regeneration of trees or shrubs and lianes and creepers have been eaten out.

game-animal production. Their scientific and aesthetic values are very high. The preservation in a natural condition of as much as possible of the unique native flora and fauna of the mountain lands is the entirely legitimate desire of many people, a desire irreconcilable with that of other people for the management of these lands for the continued production of game animals. All that can really be said at the moment is that watershed-management needs must come first. As yet we have neither the expertise nor the trained manpower to attempt integration of game animal management with watershed management in the mountain country.

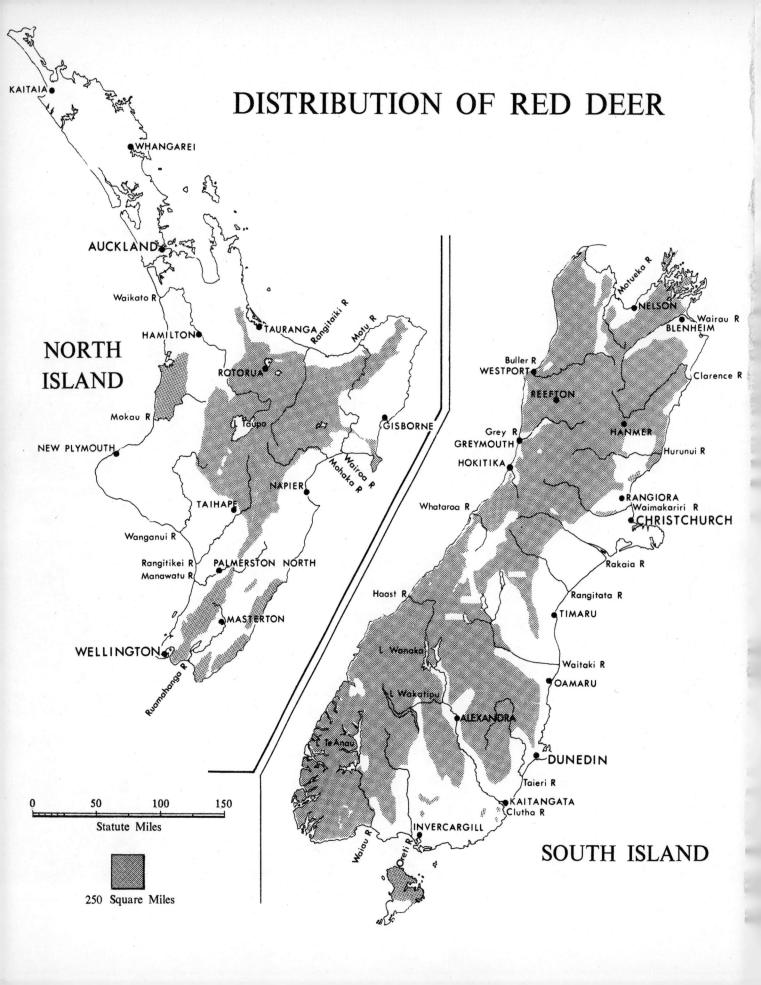

DISTRIBUTION OF RED DEER

KAITAIA

WHANGAREI

AUCKLAND

Waikato R

HAMILTON

NORTH ISLAND

TAURANGA

Rangitaiki R

Motu R

ROTORUA

Mokau R

L Taupo

GISBORNE

NEW PLYMOUTH

Wairoa R

Mohaka R

NAPIER

TAIHAPE

Wanganui R

Rangitikei R

PALMERSTON NORTH

Manawatu R

MASTERTON

WELLINGTON

Ruamahanga R

Motueka R

NELSON

Wairau R

BLENHEIM

Buller R

WESTPORT

Clarence R

REEFTON

Grey R

HANMER

GREYMOUTH

HOKITIKA

Hurunui R

Whataroa R

RANGIORA

Waimakariri R

CHRISTCHURCH

Rakaia R

Haast R

Rangitata R

TIMARU

L Wanaka

Waitaki R

L Wakatipu

OAMARU

ALEXANDRA

Te Anau

DUNEDIN

Taieri R

KAITANGATA

Clutha R

INVERCARGILL

Wairau R

Oreti R

SOUTH ISLAND

0	50	100	150

Statute Miles

250 Square Miles

Juvenile red deer stags, Canterbury high country.

PAGE 19: Red deer hinds, Forgotten Valley, Otago.

RED DEER
L. H. Harris

RED DEER *(Cervus elaphus)* are widely distributed throughout Europe, North Africa, and Asia Minor in varying degrees of abundance. They differ considerably in size, colour, and antler formation, and in eastern Europe tend to develop characteristics strongly resembling the larger wapiti, to which they are closely related.

Small herds of red deer are often kept semi-domesticated in parks, particularly in England. Animals from such parks, together with wild red deer from Scotland, were the founders of New Zealand's present herds. English park deer were also established in Australia and later brought from there to New Zealand. From the first liberation in 1851 in the Maitai Valley, Nelson, introductions from overseas by the Government and acclimatisation societies continued until about 1919. In addition there was considerable interchange of deer between the provinces from the 1880s onwards. The establishment of breeding farms by some acclimatisation societies greatly simplified the obtaining of young animals for further liberations. Illegal liberation is believed to have continued even up to recent times, despite the fact that it is regarded as a serious offence and carries heavy penalties.

Provision of sport for the early settlers that contributed a "touch of home" was the reason for red deer introductions, but once the herds became well established, the prospects of substantial licence revenue from overseas sportsmen gained importance.

The increase and spread of red deer were remarkably rapid. The important factors in this were: congenial climate, abundant food, especially winter browse, stringent prohibition in the early years of any shooting, earlier maturity and a younger breeding age in females, and the absence of predators. The rapid establishment of the species was greatly assisted by continual vigorous "planting" of animals in all the main forested areas from North Auckland to Stewart Island between the 1860s and the 1920s.

Up to the 1920s herds, though occupying vast tracts of mountainous country, maintained their identity, but soon afterwards occupation became continuous over large stretches of country. The original herds mingled and there was interbreeding among different strains. This and deterioration in the available forage have tended to produce heads of inferior quality and size. Although red deer have for many years been present throughout most of the unoccupied or sparsely settled country suitable to them, there has been continuous slow dispersal to new territory.

Red deer are to be found in almost any type of New Zealand vegetation throughout the tops, forests, scrublands, and grasslands of the mountains and on lowland pastures along the lower edges of mountain forests. There is a wide range in habitat, including the wet forests of Fiordland and Stewart Island in the far south, the dry beech forests of Canterbury and the central North Island, planted coniferous forests, and improved lowland pastures. The deer are most at home in the vast areas of South Island high country where there is a mosaic of beech forest and tussock grasslands, but they may become almost entirely forest dwellers, as in the Urewera forests of the central North Island.

At first hunting of red deer was strictly controlled by a licence system administered by acclimatisation societies, but the rapid increase in numbers and general deterioration in heads caused some societies to offer bounties and institute culling. This was first done in the Lake Hawea region, where deer had been liberated almost forty years earlier. From then on culling became more widespread in an effort to reduce the number of animals and to improve their quality. The early attempts at herd management failed miserably; numbers were already too great and herds too widely dispersed. From 1924 onwards there was a gradual removal of protection, and by 1927 protection was lifted completely in State forests.

In 1930 all protection was removed from deer and in the following year control operations were begun as a continuous activity by the Department of Internal Affairs. In the most favourable and remote habitats animals had built up to very large numbers and expert Internal Affairs Department hunters shot thousands a year. The record tally for one man on foot in one day in the early years was 101 deer; this record still stands. Operations were started principally at the request of tussock-grassland runholders, who were alarmed by deer competing with domestic stock for feed.

It was soon realised also that deer were causing extensive damage in forests and to vegetation along the mountain tops above the bush-line.

In 1956 responsibility for the control of introduced animals was transferred to the Forest Service under authority provided by the Noxious Animals Act 1956. By that time red deer had reached almost their present limits and no economic means had been found to prevent their spread. From 1931 to 1968 a total of 1,067,434 deer were destroyed by Government hunters, and although the very large and concentrated populations are no longer present today, numbers are still too high in catchments where active erosion is taking place.

In the late 1950s the emphasis in control gradually changed from maximum kill to concentration on checking the harmful effects of deer on catchments of rivers, the flooding of which was a constant threat to farms and communities in the lower reaches. Deer control has continued on this basis, one effect being that the total tallies of Government hunters have declined.

Throughout much of the deer-inhabited country not under control schemes the Forest Service encourages hunting by sportsmen by providing huts, forming and maintaining access tracks, and bridging streams and rivers.

In the past few years an export trade in venison has developed at a remarkable rate. The value of venison exported for the year ending 30 June 1971 was $4.7 million. Many of the country's most skilled hunters are engaged in this industry. The more enterprising meat hunters have extended operations into more difficult country by use of helicopters and jet boats to recover and transport carcasses. (See also section on commercialisation of wild deer, page 133).

Legislation passed in 1967 permits the farming of deer under strict conditions (see page 139). These are much the same as for ordinary farm stock, except that retaining fences must be of a prescribed standard and no species can be kept in districts where they do not occur in a wild state. Very little is yet known about deer farming.

Red deer remain the No. 1 target of thousands of sportsmen, even though the large herds consisting of a hundred or more animals have now disappeared. Most hunters can still reach red deer country within fifty miles of their homes. even if these are in large towns. Actual hunting is often over steep and broken territory, and this demands a high standard of physical fitness and judgment in following routes and recognising dangers, particularly from sudden deterioration in the weather.

Many New Zealand deerstalkers have acquired the requisite skills and endurance and have also attained a very high level of markmanship. They provide a corps of hunters with the ability to assist substantially in the overall control of deer. The range of such activities is being extended by the availability of rugged motor vehicles, charter aircraft of suitable types, and jet boats. The Forest Service is improving facilities in remote areas to encourage shooting there.

RIGHT: An adult red deer stag photographed in the Wilkin Valley, Otago. Just before and during the rut (mating season), stags wallow in mud and their necks swell, making the mane more prominent.

RIGHT: This mature red deer stag carries a promising set of antlers. Clearly shown just below the eye is the pre-orbital gland which during the rut exudes an odorous, waxy secretion.

Havelock Valley, Rangitata. Mountain vegetation and tussock grasslands of the South Island have supported very large numbers of red deer. Herbaceous plants and introduced grasses between the tussocks are good sources of food.

Cattle Flat, mid Dart Valley, Otago. In this area there is a mosaic of beech forest and tussock grassland on the eastern side of the Southern Alps. It is much favoured by red deer. Very large herds still remain in remote places.

Near Lake Lillian, Harper-Avoca district, Canterbury. Here tussock grassland is used for extensive grazing, chiefly by merino sheep. The strong competition for available fodder exerted by deer and other wild animals was the reason for their destruction being undertaken by the Government in 1931. Subsequently work was extended to the montane forests to reduce the damage being done there.

27

Forgotten Valley, Otago. A combination of open mountain tops, silver beech (*Nothofagus menziesii*) forest, and open valley, ideal for red deer. It has been colonised by them within the last twenty years.

Forgotten Valley, Otago. The interior of the forest infested with red deer. In their primitive state the silver beech trees and the forest floor were densely clothed with moss, lichens, and filmy ferns. Regeneration of trees was plentiful. The rich vegetation has been eaten out and the ground trampled and consolidated. Regeneration is now non-existent, and the future of the forest is precarious.

WAPITI
K. H. Miers

WAPITI *(Cervus canadensis)*, the elk of North America, are the largest round-horned deer in the world. Their introduction from the USA was made by the New Zealand Tourist Department in 1905, when eighteen were released at George Sound in Fiordland.

Wapiti are closely related to red deer and may be regarded, as Lydekker asserts *(Deer of All Lands,* 1898; and *The Great and Small Game of Europe, Western and Northern Asia and America,* 1901), as being the Asiatic and North American forms of the elaphine group of the genus *Cervus.* Three subspecies are recognised from Asia and six from North America. The Rocky Mountain wapiti *(Cervus canadensis nelsoni),* the largest of the North American subspecies, was liberated in New Zealand.

The wapiti throve; by 1921 they had spread south to Lake Marchant at the head of Caswell Sound and east into the Lake Hankinson — Lake Thomson country. Within a couple of years trophy hunting began and the seeds of a controversy were sown. At the time of liberation and the early period of hunting no ethical qualms were held about wapiti occupying a part of a national park. Later the area was to come under the aegis of the National Parks Act 1952 and this act simply states that: " . . . . the native flora and fauna shall as far as possible be preserved and the introduced flora and fauna shall as far as possible be exterminated".

Wapiti now occupy about a sixth of Fiordland National Park and are found to the west of Lake Te Anau and south of the Castle Mountain - Mt MacKenzie massif and north of a Bradshaw Sound - Coronation Peak line. Occasionally bulls are encountered outside the area described. To the south wapiti are hemmed in by a strongly established red deer population which seems to have provided an effective barrier to their spreading further. To the north, the high and precipitous Milford Sound and Cleddau Valley system, now much frequented by man, will almost certainly provide a northern limit to their future distribution.

Since the 1920s some thousands of New Zealand stalkers have braved the Fiordland terrain, sandflies, and weather in pursuit of trophy heads. Bruce Banwell in a recent comprehensive account of wapiti hunting in New Zealand lists eighty-five heads as exceeding fifty inches in either length or spread. It seems appropriate to note that some of the early New Zealand heads are as big as those recorded for North America, where the record books detail several in excess of sixty inches in length and some that approach that figure in spread.

Mention has been made of the close relationship of wapiti and red deer. Many sportsmen have reported hybrids from time to time. In the late 1940s efforts were made to "cull" the wapiti area of red deer and suspected hybrids. Indeed these endeavours continue to the present day. In 1948 a comprehensive expedition was mounted to investigate the wapiti area. It included Dr Olaus J. Murie, an acknowledged expert on the Rocky Mountain wapiti, who carried out a detailed examination of red deer hybridisation. Dr Murie was able to state conclusively that hybridisation was occurring, but was unable to indicate the extent of hybrids in the population. Research by Forest Service biologists should shortly give an answer.

The wapiti in New Zealand occupy terrain steeper than that from which the animals came in North America. The hard rock, glacially dissected Fiordland area provided a habitat where cliffs and steep valley sides effectively channelled the dispersal of wapiti from George Sound. Indeed, the Katherine and Edith Valleys at the head of the sound were soon occupied and these led the colonising herd into the Wapiti River and Glaisnock and Stillwater Valleys. However, the nearby Lugarburn was not colonised until the mid 1930s, and ten years or more were to elapse before the beasts found a way through the cliffs into the Midburn. Likewise, other eastern valleys and some of the seaward peninsulas between the fiords were occupied between 1940 and 1950. What is probably the last chance for wapiti to move into unoccupied country has been the colonising of an area north of Sutherland Sound which began a few years ago.

The vegetation of Fiordland is greatly influenced by heavy rainfall, cool summer temperatures, and impoverished soil. The forests are dominated by silver beech *(Nothofagus menziesii),* with some areas where mountain beech *(N. solandri* var. *cliffortioides)* is important. At low elevations near the sea or lakes there may be rimu *(Dacrydium cupressinum)* and, mainly on the valley sides, southern rata *(Metrosideros umbellata).* Above the bushline at about 3,000 feet is a discontinuous zone of scrub including the species *Olearia colensoi, O. crosby-smithiana, Dracophyllum, Hebe, Neopanax colensoi,* and *Phormium colensoi.* Above the subalpine scrub is a grassland and herb field zone which is dominated by snow grasses, mainly *Chionochloa flavescens, C. pallens, C. crassiuscula, C. teretifolia,* and *C. acicularis.*

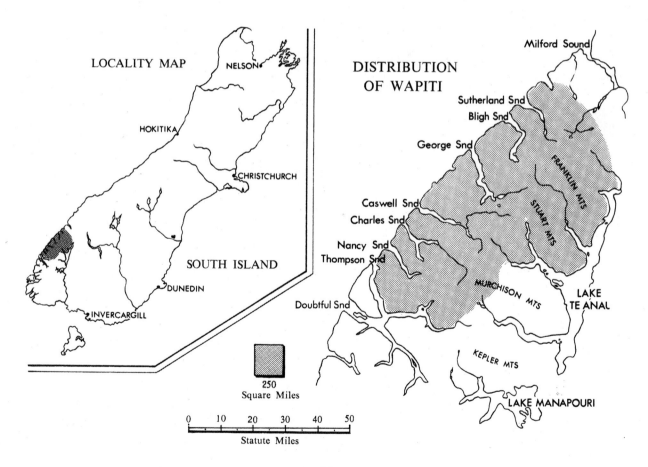

LOCALITY MAP

NELSON

HOKITIKA

CHRISTCHURCH

SOUTH ISLAND

DUNEDIN

INVERCARGILL

250 Square Miles

0 10 20 30 40 50
Statute Miles

DISTRIBUTION OF WAPITI

Milford Sound

Sutherland Snd

Bligh Snd

George Snd

FRANKLIN MTS

STUART MTS

Caswell Snd

Charles Snd

Nancy Snd

Thompson Snd

MURCHISON MTS

LAKE TE ANAL

Doubtful Snd

KEPLER MTS

LAKE MANAPOURI

31

A wapiti cow and her calf at the headwaters of the Pitt River, Fiordland National Park.
The prominent, light-coloured rump patch is clearly visible.

RIGHT: A wapiti bull feeding above the bushline in the Edith Valley, Fiordland National Park. A close cousin of the common red deer, wapiti are much larger, sometimes standing 5 ft high at the shoulder and weighing up to 700 lb. Although slowly extending their range in New Zealand, their movements are restricted by the steep-walled glacial valleys of Fiordland, which form natural barriers.

Mount Pluvius, an example of the magnificent scenery of the Fiordland mountain tops. It is dangerous country, even for wild animals. Their skeletons are frequently found below bluffs.

Looking down the Edith River to Lake Alice in the distance, near where wapiti were first liberated in 1905 in George Sound, Fiordland. Typical Fiordland wapiti habitat. Here ice-worn rocks had U-shaped glaciated valleys carved through them during the last glaciation. Valley floors and sides are covered with silver beech (*Nothofagus menziesii*) and southern rata (*Metrosideros umbellata*) forest growing precariously on the smooth rocks. Above the timber-line, at 1,500–2,000 ft from the valley floors, alpine vegetation dominated by grasses replaces forest. Rainfall is 200–300 in. a year or higher. Snow lies on the tops most of the winter.

Looking up Worsley Valley, Fiordland. A typical U-shaped valley formed by a glacier. The very steep sides, 1,500–2,000 ft high, present barriers to the spread of wapiti and have preserved some valleys.

RIGHT: Silver beech (*Nothofagus menziesii*) forest interior in the Large Burn, near Lake Marchant, at the head of Caswell Sound, Fiordland. The dense, tangled shrub and fern growth and the thick covering of moss and lichen are characteristic of the forest in its primitive condition.

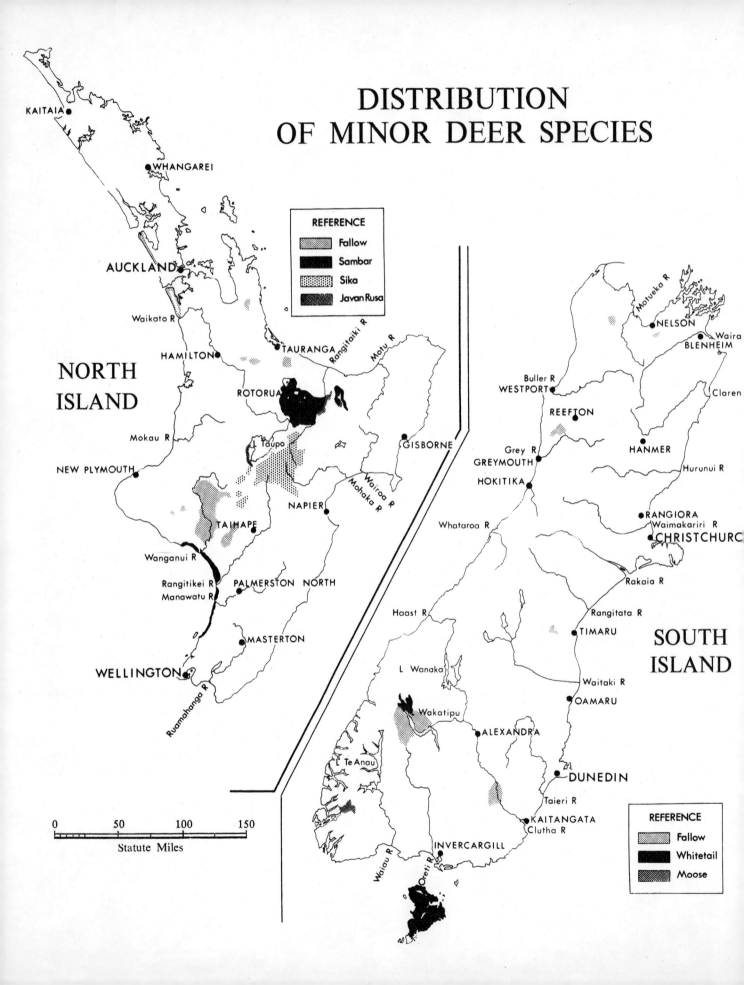

DISTRIBUTION
OF MINOR DEER SPECIES

REFERENCE
- Fallow
- Sambar
- Sika
- Javan Rusa

REFERENCE
- Fallow
- Whitetail
- Moose

NORTH ISLAND

KAITAIA

WHANGAREI

AUCKLAND

Waikato R

HAMILTON

TAURANGA

Rangitaiki R

Motu R

ROTORUA

GISBORNE

Mokau R

L. Taupo

NEW PLYMOUTH

Wairoa R

Mahaka R

NAPIER

TAIHAPE

Wanganui R

Rangitikei R

Manawatu R

PALMERSTON NORTH

MASTERTON

WELLINGTON

Ruamahanga R

0   50   100   150
Statute Miles

SOUTH ISLAND

Motueka R

NELSON

Waira
BLENHEIM

Buller R
WESTPORT

Claren

REEFTON

HANMER

Grey R
GREYMOUTH

Hurunui R

HOKITIKA

RANGIORA
Waimakariri R
CHRISTCHURC

Whataroa R

Rakaia R

Haast R

Rangitata R

TIMARU

L. Wanaka

Waitaki R

OAMARU

Wakatipu

ALEXANDRA

DUNEDIN

L. Te Anau

Taieri R

KAITANGATA
Clutha R

Waiau R

Oreti R

INVERCARGILL

RUSA DEER
L. H. Harris

RUSA DEER *(Cervus timoriensis)* occur as the smallest, most localised group of deer in New Zealand. They are native to parts of South-east Asia, including Timor, Java, the Moluccas, and the Celebes. They have been introduced into New Caledonia, New Guinea, Borneo, and Australia. Their importation here from New Caledonia in 1907 was made in the belief that they were sambar deer, and it was not until 1955 that the small localised herd in the Galatea foothills (Rotorua district) was identified as being Javan rusa. Even today many of the older people in the Galatea area refer to these deer as the "little sambar".

The general appearance is similar to that of sambar, but the rusa are much smaller. Furthermore, they are distinguishable by their smaller ears, white chin, front, and underparts, and a thinner tail, tufted at the end. Rusa antlers generally carry only six points and are attractive and distinctive. The terminal tines are usually of unequal length, and, the rear one is generally regarded as a continuation of the main beam.

The relatively restricted area they occupy consists of dense manuka, fern, and toetoe. A few animals have been observed in the forest interior, but the majority are scrub-dwellers and show preference for remaining near cultivated land. They use the scrub faces and patches of fern and swamp to rest in during the day, and at night they work their way on to nearby farms to feed on crops and pasture. Because of their semi-nocturnal habits, extreme wariness and timidity, and also their small numbers, rusa rank high as a big-game trophy in New Zealand.

The rusa create some problems because of their liking for farm crops, but they do not pose any serious threat to forests. They have, however, produced widespread systems of tunnel-like tracks through marginal scrub faces, making favourable habitat for opossums, which have not been slow to take full advantage of this.

Displaying some of the stealth and cunning for which they are noted, this wild rusa hind and calf were caught by the flashgun as they sneaked along a fenceline. The eyes appear prominently white due to the angle of the flashlight. Along the Galatea plain and foothills the deer have adopted semi-nocturnal habits and frequently visit crop paddocks bordering the forest during their night-time foraging.

RIGHT: A mature rusa stag. Although closely related to red deer, rusa have a distinctive antler formation and wider and larger ears, more like their bigger cousins the sambar deer.

BELOW: Rusa deer have the most limited distribution of all the deer species established in New Zealand. This rusa calf was photographed near the north-western boundary of the Urewera National Park, where there is a small herd.

A juvenile rusa stag (*left*) and an adult hind. This remarkable photograph was taken at night with flash equipment. Rusa are semi-nocturnal and frequent neighbouring farm crops during the night, returning to the sanctuary of dense scrub before daybreak.

Rusa deer habitat. Bracken fern and scrub country in Urewera National Park. There is a small, slowly-spreading herd of rusa deer in the east of the lower Rangitaiki River valley.

SAMBAR DEER
L. H. Harris

AFTER WAPITI second largest of the deer in New Zealand, sambar *(Cervus unicolor)* have the reputation of being the most cunning and the least seen. Native to India, Ceylon, and parts of Southeast Asia, this large (up to 500 lb) deer was introduced into New Zealand in 1875, when a pair were privately liberated near the mouth of the Rangitikei River, Manawatu, North Island. The resulting herd established itself along the narrow western coastal strip between Otaki and Wanganui, which remains the extent of the herd's range today. Between 1880 and 1921 calves from the Manawatu herd were captured and sent to other North Island districts for liberation. As a consequence of this, small, scattered herds now exist in the Taupo-Rotorua region and near Whakatane.

Essentially forest-loving creatures in their native lands, they have readily adapted to a variety of habitat types in both the Manawatu and Rotorua areas, ranging from raupo swamp - lupin - manuka along the Manawatu coast to exotic-pine plantations and even dense indigenous forests in the central North Island. This colonisation has occurred unhindered, despite increasing agricultural activity and human disturbance. Sambar are noted for their general disregard for nearby human activity. It is not uncommon for them to live permanently near human habitation; they have been observed to remain secluded near forest workers operating bulldozers and chainsaws, only to slip stealthily away during a brief lull in activity. Because of this inherent stealth and cunning, plus their semi-nocturnal habits, sambar are considered by many sportsmen to be the ultimate big-game trophy. However, their extremely limited numbers and the difficulty of access to sambar territory, much of which is private property, generally put the animal beyond the hopes of most hunters.

The diet of sambar, like that of its smaller cousin the red deer, varies considerably according to habitat. Stomach analyses have shown a wide variety of vegetation including flax, various grasses, swedes, and leaves of some of the indigenous trees. Sambar will graze pastures and crops very readily. Deer living within or near exotic pine forests show a strong liking for terminal buds and bark of radiata pine. Bark-biting has also been observed on alder saplings. Their penchant for radiata pine bark does not endear them to the forester; in some districts damage by sambar to young plantations has been severe. They appear to damage only the young, smooth bark before it becomes thick, furrowed, and woody and prefer trees about five to six years old. The bark will sometimes be stripped off up to about seven feet and often a large number of trees will be damaged during one feeding. Although the trees seldom die, a substantial portion of the butt log becomes sap-stained and useless for timber production. Antler thrashing also occurs to a limited extent.

The breeding habits of sambar deer in New Zealand have never been clearly defined, nor has any comprehensive study of the species been undertaken. From the limited evidence available it would appear that there is little or no vocal roar such as is characteristic with stags of some other deer species during the rut. In addition, since hinds carrying embryos have been shot during most months of the year, it would seem that rutting is without pronounced or clearly defined seasons and may take place over the greater part of the year. Sambar calves, unlike the offspring of most other deer, are not spotted at birth. Because stags may be found in velvet at any time of the year, there may be some truth in the popular belief that sambar stags do not cast their antlers annually but retain them for two, or even three, years.

RIGHT: A large-bodied sambar deer stag in the Rotorua district. Note the large, rounded ears that are a distinguishing feature of the species, as are the antlers, which lack bez tines.

A study in motion—giving the impression of being a miniture *Cardigan Bay*, this attractive sambar calf could one day become a massive 500 lb stag. Unlike the offspring of other deer species, sambar calves are not spotted at birth.

LEFT: An adult sambar hind. In New Zealand the species has adapted well to widely varying habitats—from the coastal sand-dunes and swamp of the Manawatu to the dense indigenous forest of the Urewera and even the exotic pine forests of Kaingaroa.

Sand-dunes on the west coast of the North Island near Bulls, where sambar live. These dunes are covered with vegetation dominated by yellow lupin (*Lupinus arboreus*), cabbage tree (*Cordyline australis*), and sand-dune grasses, and are therefore stable.

LEFT: Damage by sambar to radiata pine. Sambar strip the bark in young plantations of radiata pine and sometimes of other exotic species. This creates a permanent defect in the most valuable part of the tree.

49

FALLOW DEER
L. H. Harris

THE NATIVE HOME of fallow deer (*Dama dama*) is southern Europe, parts of Asia Minor, and limited areas in north-west Africa. Like other species of deer, they can become semi-domesticated and, as such, tend to rely on human care and assistance, particularly with winter feeding. This characteristic has made the fallow deer an attractive subject for introduction and acclimatisation in many countries. As a result they are now to be found in the USA, Australia, Chile, Denmark, central and northern Europe, and even on an isolated island of the Fiji group.

Their introduction into New Zealand began in 1864 with three animals from Richmond Park, Surrey, England, which were liberated in Nelson. In the following decade many more fallow deer were imported and released in numerous localities throughout the country. Today herds have become established in at least thirteen separate localities. The largest and best known of these are the Blue Mountains herd near Tapanui, the Lake Wakatipu herds, and Paparoa herd of northern Westland, and the Wanganui herd in the North Island.

Considerably smaller than the average mature red deer stag, a full-grown fallow buck seldom exceeds three feet in height at the shoulder. The most obvious difference between the males of the two species is the flattened or palmated antlers of the fallow. On the main beam, before palmation begins, are brow and trez tines. (Like the sika, fallow bucks do not have bez tines.) Palmation of the antlers generally begins at about three years of age and maximum antler growth is reached at six to nine years. When full palmation is achieved, the rearmost edge of the antlers carries a number of small points, called spillers.

Fallow deer have a wide colour variation, more so than other species, and in both sexes may be found animals from white to almost jet black. Usually, however, the summer skin is a light brown or fawn with small white spots spread over the back, upper sides, and haunches. A dark, almost black, stripe runs along the backbone to the tail. The belly, inside the upper portions of the legs, under the tail, and the rump below the tail are white or cream. The tail, between seven and eight inches long, is proportionately much longer than that of red deer. In winter the pelage generally changes to a much darker brown and the spots all but disappear. However, the Wanganui and Blue Mountains herds consist predominantly of the so-called black fallow that have an even sooty-chocolate pelage with little or no trace of spots.

Fallow deer are gregarious animals that tend to remain in herds throughout the year. Herds become very dense, especially when left relatively undisturbed. Intensive shooting, however, disrupts the herd structure, and the animals then disperse in small groups; some even become "loners". Fallow utilise their range completely and seldom move far unless pushed by hunting pressure. Because of general reluctance to extend their range unless pressed they are slow colonisers of territory compared with red deer. Nevertheless, they are the second most widespread deer species in New Zealand, and the herds continue to spread slowly through suitable habitat.

Showing a marked preference for lowland areas such as river flats and lower valley sides, fallow deer do not generally utilise the subalpine scrub or open tussock tops as do red deer. Exceptions to this rule, however, are the Lake Wakatipu and Blue Mountains animals, which are sometimes forced up to the bushline when snow at lower altitudes covers their food supplies. There is little indication of any fixed seasonal movement elsewhere, although some animals occasionally follow the spring growth.

Having colonised only those areas close to the original points of liberation, fallow deer have not assumed the pest proportions of red deer. Nonetheless, spasmodic control operations against the Caples herd in the Lake Wakatipu district and Blue Mountains herd have been necessary in recent years — particularly the latter herd, which has caused damage in plantings of young exotic trees in and around the Tapanui district.

The fallow buck, with its attractive palmated antlers and fine skin, has always ranked high as a trophy animal with New Zealand hunters. With the ever-increasing hunting pressure being applied to the separate herds by sportsmen and the recent boom in venison recovery, from which the fallow have not been excluded, it is unlikely that the species will ever again become a pest, except perhaps on a minor, local scale.

RIGHT: A mature fallow deer buck showing the distinctive, moose-like, palmated antlers.

The long tail of this adult fallow doe is a distinguishing feature; it is proportionately much longer than that of red deer. This doe shows the white spots of her summer coat.

RIGHT: Fallow deer in the Caples Valley, Lake Wakatipu, where they are plentiful. They graze on the valley floor and browse in the beech forests on the lower slopes. They rarely enter the alpine vegetation above the forest. The herds are spreading slowly.

52

An attractive fallow deer fawn.

LEFT: The interior of the beech forest shown on page 53. The vegetation within reach has been eaten out by sheep, fallow deer, and hares. The forest floor has been thoroughly trampled.

OVERLEAF
A broad view of Caples Valley, Otago. The most distant clearing is the area depicted on page 53.

SIKA DEER
L. H. Harris

SIKA DEER *(Cervus nippon)*, also known as Japanese deer, were introduced and liberated near Oamaru in 1885. Although the animals lived and bred for a short time, they eventually disappeared, and it is suspected that they were exterminated by local residents. In 1905 a successful release of sika was made on the edge of the Kaimanawa Range, near Lake Taupo. The animals came from an English park herd, and although they are recorded as being of the Manchurian sub-species, present evidence suggests that we have a sika herd of somewhat mixed parentage. Sika subspecies readily interbreed, and even crosses with red deer have been noted.

Sika occur naturally in Japan, Formosa, and northern China, where many herds are kept in parks. They have been introduced into a number of countries besides New Zealand, including Australia, the USA, Denmark, the USSR, Germany, and France. Their present range in the central North Island extends from Tongariro National Park and the northern Ruahine Range to Kaingaroa State Forest and Maungaharuru Range. They continue to spread slowly, inhabiting new territory, and, like other species of deer in New Zealand, have been shot or observed far outside their known range, the areas including Te Kuiti, Mokai-Patea Range, Wakarara Range, and the Wairarapa. Their habitat is mixed beech *(Nothofagus* spp.) forest and also large tracts of native grasses and scrublands.

People sometimes find difficulty in distinguishing between red and sika deer, so brief mention of some of the main identifying features may be of use. Sika are smaller and lighter in build than red deer; a mature sika stag is approximately thirty-five inches high at the shoulder, and a mature male red often attains about forty-five inches. The sika hind, as with females of other deer species, is considerably smaller than the stag and seldom exceeds thirty-two inches in shoulder height. The tail of a sika deer is longer than that of a red deer, is white underneath and has a black stripe. The belly is whitish as is the distinctive heart-shaped rump patch, which is bordered with a thin band of black hair. One of the more striking characteristics of the sika is the attractive rich red-brown coat, which in summer is covered with white or creamy spots. In winter the spots tend to fade and the overall colour changes to a uniform brownish grey. The typical mature sika stag carries antlers with only eight points, four on each side; in contrast to red deer, the sika has no bez tine.

From all accounts, New Zealand sika appear to have produced larger antlers than their original forbears. This is typical of most of the deer species introduced from overseas and now successfully acclimatised. A congenial climate, ample food, and complete protection for many years are doubtless some of the reasons for the often spectacular antler growth.

Because of its attractiveness, cunning, and relatively restricted distribution, the sika is highly regarded as a trophy animal. Compared with red deer, sika are elusive and considerably more difficult to hunt with success.

Although sika deer are not naturally nocturnal, they will remain in seclusion until nightfall when subjected to constant and intensive disturbances. If left relatively undisturbed they will often graze in the open grasslands for long periods during most hours of daylight. This is particularly so towards spring, when fresh plant growth is more abundant. Sika deer are not generally found at higher altitudes, but during winter they may utilise sheltered, sunny sites at mid-forest level. Where sika and red deer occur together the sika generally maintain better physical condition. This appears to be due to the fact that sika are more efficient and intensive foragers.

For a number of years after the Second World War sika deer were the subject of Government shooting operations aimed at reducing their numbers and checking their rate of dispersal. Nowadays, control measures against the sika herds are sporadic because the animals have spread into country already occupied and modified by red deer. Control operations are not aimed at particular species, but rather at all deer populations to reduce numbers to a manageable level.

The antlers of this mature sika deer stag are in their final stages of development and soon the soft velvet covering will die and be stripped off.

Of the deer introduced into New Zealand many have produced larger antlers than their ancestors. This sika stag photographed in the Kaimanawa Range is one such animal; its antlers probably exceed all known world records.

The Oamaru Valley close to the headwaters of the Mohaka River in the Kaimanawa Range, near where the first successful liberation of sika deer took place. Scrub growth of native species and grasses, native and introduced, occupy the valley floor. The forest is beech. The scrub belt is excellent cover for sika deer, which have largely displaced the once plentiful red deer in the locality.

A sika stag interrupted in its feeding in the Oamaru Valley, Kaimanawa Range, North Island.

Sika deer stags, Oamaru Valley. The one with the collar is in winter coat, the other still in its summer coat. The collar was put on by a device placed on a deer trail which snaps it on to the animal without its being captured. Movements of animals thus marked are observed in the course of studies of their behaviour.

WHITETAIL DEER
L. H. Harris

WHITETAIL, OR VIRGINIA DEER *(Odocoileus virginianus)* are indigenous to the American continent from Canada, through the USA and Mexico, to Peru and Bolivia. Throughout this region the animal varies considerably in size and colour; there is also a wide range of habitats. Generalising, one may say that the further south the deer occur, the smaller they are. In the north, whitetail may weigh as much as 300 pounds and stand nearly 40 inches at the shoulder. In contrast, in Mexico it seldom weighs more than 40 to 50 pounds. In New Zealand the male whitetail averages between 130 and 150 pounds, and the female is generally under 100 pounds.

Whitetail deer were first introduced into New Zealand in 1901. Four animals were released in the Takaka Valley, Nelson, but the liberation was not a success. A further attempt to establish them was made in 1905, when the Government purchased whitetail deer in the United States and shipped them to New Zealand. Of this importation, nine animals were released on Stewart Island (Port Pegasus) and a further nine in the Rees Valley north from Lake Wakatipu. These liberations were successful, and whitetail deer are now found in both areas, although much more plentiful on Stewart Island.

The Lake Wakatipu herd has never extended its range much, nor has the population thrived. In fact, it can be said that the herd is steadily declining and may disappear in a few years. Natural mortality in the area is high and it is thought that the environment is not entirely suitable. The remnant of the herd is a popular tourist attraction, and animals can sometimes be seen grazing at the bush edges close to farms and roads. Studies have been undertaken to determine whether there is a biological reason for the decline over recent years.

By contrast the Stewart Island herd has flourished and at times it has been necessary to take measures to reduce the overall population of deer — red and whitetail. However, the latter, because of their timidity, wariness, and use of dense cover, are difficult to hunt on this rugged, heavily forested island. The range of whitetail deer on Stewart Island is restricted largely to coastal fringes and seldom extends more than half a mile inland. Animals are sometimes seen on remote sandy beaches, where they forage for seaweed. There is no overland access to many parts of the coastal strip that whitetail deer frequent, and approach by sea can be hazardous.

An extremely attractive deer with somewhat delicate facial features, the whitetail is also called the Virginia deer. Most hunters consider the former name more apt because of the animal's habit of holding its large tail erect like a white flag when alarmed. The conspicuous tail, twelve to fifteen inches long and lined underneath with white hair, is said to guide fawns as parents flee through dense undergrowth.

The typical summer coat of the whitetail is rich coppery red; it darkens to brownish grey with the onset of winter. The belly and throat are white and the muzzle and eyes are ringed with white. The buck's antler formation is distinctive, the main beam curving forward, with the tines rising vertically from it. There is no brow tine.

Fawns, born in December and January, are spotted at birth and retain their attractive marking for three to four months. In North America whitetail does living under favourable conditions often have twins and sometimes triplets, but in New Zealand a single offspring appears to be usual.

The whitetail buck, unlike the red deer, does not roar during the mating season. In fact both sexes usually remain silent until disturbed. As these deer have extremely acute senses of sight, hearing, and smell, they are difficult to stalk successfully. Often the hunter will be rewarded only by a sharp snort and the sight of a "white flag" as the deer bounds into thick cover.

A mature whitetail buck showing the delicate facial features, large tail, and forward-curving antlers (in velvet) that are distinctive features of the species. Lower Dart Valley, Otago.

Typical antler formation of a whitetail buck.

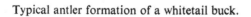

65

Whitetail deer are timid and stealthy. On Stewart Island, where they are sometimes referred to as "the little grey ghosts", they provide hunters with a real test of stalking ability.

A whitetail doe. The conspicuous tail, which is some 12 in. long and lined underneath with long white hair, is held erect like a flag when the deer is alarmed. It is said that it also acts as a guide for juveniles to follow when the parent flees through dense forest.

The whitetail deer herd in the Dart Valley, Lake Wakatipu, has remained small. Beech forest covers the valley sides. Introduced and native grasses grow on the valley floor. These deer do not wander to the mountain tops.

Two successful liberations of whitetail deer were made in very different types of country. One was on Stewart Island. Part of it is illustrated. The deer have spread through dense, wet, mixed broadleaf evergreen forest.

OTHER INTRODUCED DEER
L. H. Harris

FOLLOWING are details of four other species of deer that were brought to New Zealand. Only one, the moose, may still exist.

MOOSE. The largest members of the deer families, moose *(Alces americana)*, are native to Canada, the northern USA, and northern Europe (where they are known as elk). The long-legged, ungainly animal is readily identified by its ponderous bulk, long drooping nose, a pendulous growth called the "bell" hanging from the neck of males, and the large, palmated antlers of that sex. Often reaching a height of over six feet at the shoulder and weighing up to 1,600 pounds, a mature bull is an impressive sight.

The introduction of moose to New Zealand at the turn of the century was hailed as a triumph in acclimatisation. Two liberations were made, the first in 1901 near the Hokitika Gorge, failing. A further attempt was made in March 1910, when ten moose (four bulls and six cows) obtained in Saskatchewan, Canada, were liberated at Supper Cove (Dusky Sound) in Fiordland National Park. Immediately after release two of the animals began to fight and a cow had a leg broken. Whether the injured beast disappeared or was found and destroyed is not recorded in documents that are still available.

Moose never extended their range much in the area where they were liberated or flourished. For some time it has been generally accepted that the population has steadily declined, and the species may soon be extinct. The steep-sided glacial valleys of Fiordland covered with dense forest and subjected to a rainfall of more than 200 inches are not a very suitable habitat for moose. Since the first moose hunting season opened in 1923 only three bulls have been taken by licensed stalkers, the last being shot in 1954 in Wet Jacket Arm. Despite substantially greater human activity in the Dusky Sound area in recent years there have been no authenticated sightings of moose. They have been the only wild herd in the Southern Hemisphere.

species may soon be extinct. The steep-sided MULE DEER. The mule deer *(Odocoileus hemionus)* is a native of North America. It is about the same size as the whitetail (or Virginia) deer but heavier and more solidly built. Its chief charac-teristics are forward-swept antlers carrying forked tines, large ears (hence its name), and black-tipped tail. A number of the deer were imported and released in New Zealand, the first in 1877, when eleven animals were liberated by the Auckland Acclimatisation Society near Mercer and Piako in the North Island. Neither of these liberations was successful, the animals being killed by Maoris and settlers. A further attempt at introduction was made when the Tourist Department released five animals near Tarawera, Hawke's Bay, in 1905. Although the herd was reported to be increasing ten years later, no animals have been sighted for many years and it is thought that they were eliminated by local residents before becoming established.

AXIS DEER. The axis deer *(Cervus axis)* is also known by its native name chital (spotted). This most attractive deer is indigenous to India and Ceylon. It has reddish-fawn pelage profusely covered with white spots, which are in evidence all year and in all age groups. The first axis deer were introduced as far back as 1867, when seven animals were imported from Melbourne and released in the Goodwin Bush, near Palmerston in Otago. Although the herd flourished for a time, it was eventually shot out by settlers, reportedly because of damage caused to crops. Other liberations were made on Kapiti Island and Quail Island and in Tongariro National Park and Dusky Sound. Records indicate that none of these liberations survived more than a few years; and because there have been no authenticated sightings for about fifty years, the species may be considered extinct in New Zealand.

GUEMAL. A little-known importation is that of guemal *(Hippocamelus bisulcus)*, a thickly coated medium-size deer which is at home in the high Andes of central and southern Chile. A migratory species which utilises lower-altitude forests in winter, guemal would probably have been quite at home in the Southern Alps had it been introduced there in sufficient numbers to become established. Apart from mentioning the receipt of three animals landed at Auckland in 1870, available records do not give any indication of their ultimate destination or fate.

CHAMOIS
A. H. Christie

THE GRACEFUL AND AGILE CHAMOIS *(Rupicapra rupicapra)* are carefully protected in their native habitat areas in the mountains of central Europe, because popularity as a hunting prize once heavily reduced their numbers. This popularity was also the reason for their introduction into New Zealand. First suggested in 1888, and given financial backing the following year by the Government, the project was long delayed because of difficulty in obtaining any animals. Success came when a high-ranking Austrian naval officer, well pleased by kindness shown him on a visit here and by assistance given him in obtaining specimens of our native flora and fauna, undertook to inform his Emperor of New Zealand's wish to establish chamois.

In 1907 a large roundup of chamois was carried out at the direction of Emperor Franz Josef, and from the several hundred animals gathered two males and six females were selected for shipment to New Zealand. On arrival here in March of the same year the animals were released in the vicinity of Mt Cook. They quickly adapted themselves, and increases in the herd were soon being reported.

Franz Josef's continued interest in the herd led to his sending three tame animals, a male and two females, from the grounds of Schonbrunn Palace in December 1913. (Attempts to round up more wild ones had proved too injurious to the animals). One of the does died on the way out. After an arduous journey the other animals were released, again in the Mt Cook region, in mid-1914. The doe disappeared, and was generally believed to have joined the herd; the buck remained close to the liberation point, but eventually became such a nuisance to tourists that he was shot.

By 1919 there was a report of a herd of seventy chamois near Mt Cook. Today, breeding populations are found as far north as Lake Rotoiti, in Nelson, and south to Lake Wakatipu, and they are still actively colonising the mountains, particularly in northern Fiordland. Their wide dispersal — the established populations extend 220 miles north and 120 miles south of the original liberation point — is due to the vast extent of suitable habitat unoccupied by any other mam-

This close-up clearly shows the light-coloured facial mask and symmetrical, slender horns which are found on both sexes.

mals. These herds are the only wild ones in existence outside the native habitat in central Europe.

In appearance chamois are similar to goats but have longer legs, a more erect neck, and pointed ears. They also differ in the shape and curvature of the horns. Adult males have a shoulder height of about thirty-six inches and weigh up to one hundred pounds, or sometimes more. Colour of coat varies with the season — brown to almost black in winter, and a brownish-fawn in summer. The head is a pale fawn, with a dark flash beginning near the nose, surrounding the eyes, and ending at the base of the ears and horns. The horns are the most characteristic feature and are carried by the females as well as the males. They grow almost vertically and curve near the ends to form sharp hooks. The animals' nimble-

(continued on page 74)

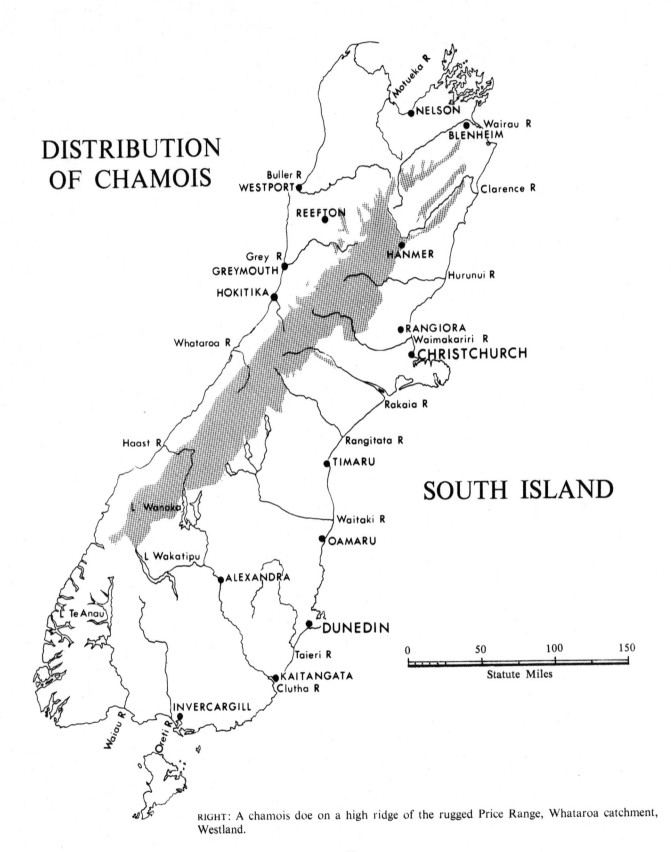

DISTRIBUTION
OF CHAMOIS

Motueka R

NELSON

Wairau R
BLENHEIM

Buller R
WESTPORT

Clarence R

REEFTON

Grey R
GREYMOUTH

HANMER

HOKITIKA

Hurunui R

Whataroa R

RANGIORA
Waimakariri R
CHRISTCHURCH

Rakaia R

Haast R

Rangitata R

TIMARU

SOUTH ISLAND

L Wanaka

Waitaki R
OAMARU

L Wakatipu

ALEXANDRA

L Te Anau

DUNEDIN

Taieri R

KAITANGATA
Clutha R

INVERCARGILL

Waiau R

Oreti R

0	50	100	150

Statute Miles

RIGHT: A chamois doe on a high ridge of the rugged Price Range, Whataroa catchment, Westland.

72

ness and surefootedness are well known. They can negotiate steep rocky faces with ease, and often at considerable speed.

The chamois move in herds, although the males separate from the body of the herd (females and young animals) when they are two to three years old. During the rut, which takes place in May and sometimes extends into June, the males move around extensively and become aggressive. Pregnancy lasts from 160 to 200 days, and the young are born in December or January. Usually one kid is born, twins occasionally. The kids are very active almost from birth.

There are no predators of chamois in New Zealand, but the rugged nature of their environment exacts some toll, mainly in winter. Young chamois in particular are often found dead at the foot of sheer rock faces or amongst avalanche debris.

Habitat favoured is grass sward close to rocky outcrops. They retreat to the rocks when the weather is bad or when disturbed. A typical day usually finds them sitting until the morning sun strikes; they then get up and start feeding. They will feed for about four hours, usually moving downslope, after which they will select a vantage point to sit and ruminate. Two or three hours before dark they will begin to feed once more, slowly moving upslope. During the night they bed down again. The pattern does not vary with the seasons, except that the vertical drift when feeding is not so evident in winter.

The bulk of the chamois diet consists of various types of grasses. In winter, though, they eat more shrub foliage because it is more generally available when snow falls over the feeding areas. When chamois browse shrubs for long periods considerable damage is done.

Control operations against chamois started in 1936, and between then and 1968 over 82,000 animals were killed by Government hunters. Sportsmen have also accounted for a large number each year.

The first chamois liberated in New Zealand were a gift from the Emperor Franz Josef of Austria in 1907. They quickly adapted themselves to their new habitat in the region of Mount Cook. This nimble-footed buck was photographed in the Harper-Avoca catchment, Canterbury.

Cupola Basin at the head of the Travers River, Nelson Lakes National Park, used as a research area for the study of chamois

PREVIOUS PAGE
A small mob of chamois fleeing across the snow-covered lower slopes of the Malte Brun Range, near Mt Cook.

The head of this Canterbury alpine valley is typical of the habitat favoured by chamois. Harper-Avoca Forest.

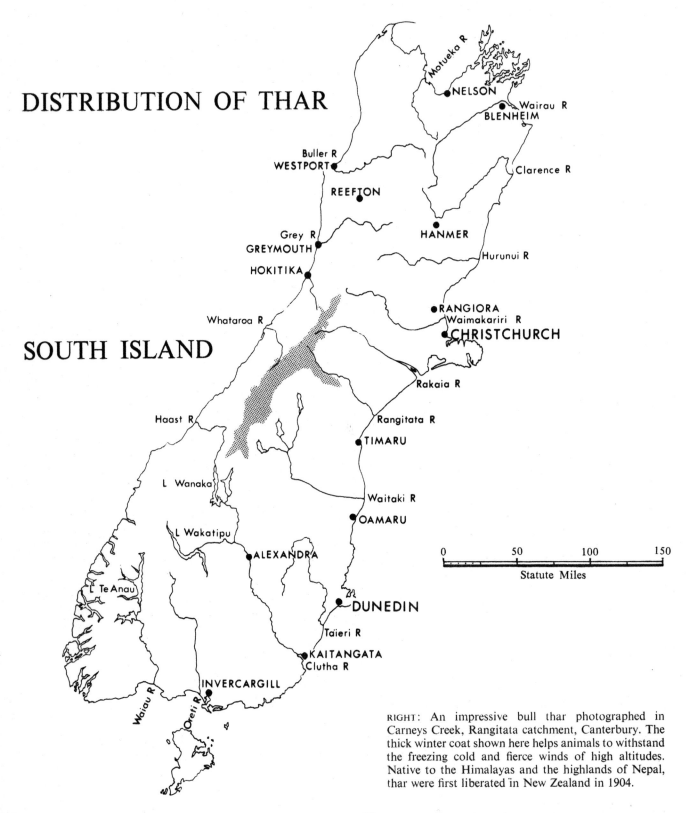

DISTRIBUTION OF THAR

SOUTH ISLAND

Motueka R

NELSON

Wairau R

BLENHEIM

Buller R

WESTPORT

Clarence R

REEFTON

Grey R

GREYMOUTH

HANMER

Hurunui R

HOKITIKA

Whataroa R

RANGIORA

Waimakariri R

CHRISTCHURCH

Rakaia R

Haast R

Rangitata R

L Wanaka

TIMARU

L Wakatipu

Waitaki R

OAMARU

ALEXANDRA

L Te Anau

DUNEDIN

Taïeri R

KAITANGATA

Clutha R

INVERCARGILL

Waiau R

Oreti R

0   50   100   150

Statute Miles

RIGHT: An impressive bull thar photographed in Carneys Creek, Rangitata catchment, Canterbury. The thick winter coat shown here helps animals to withstand the freezing cold and fierce winds of high altitudes. Native to the Himalayas and the highlands of Nepal, thar were first liberated in New Zealand in 1904.

THAR
L. H. Harris

THE THAR, or Himalayan mountain goat *(Hemitragus jemlahicus)* occurs naturally along approximately 1,600 miles of the Indian Himalayan mountain chain, where its preference for steep, rocky country takes it up to altitudes of 10,000 feet or more. The present New Zealand herd and a few animals near Capetown, South Africa, are believed to be the only herds in a wild state outside the thar's native India and Nepal.

Between 1904 and 1909 the Government imported thirteen animals from an English parkland herd and released them near Mt Cook. These introductions were successful and thar are now to be found at high altitudes along approximately 140 miles of the Southern Alps, from the Hunter Valley at the head of Lake Hawea in the south to the perimeter of the Waimakariri catchment. Thar now live on both the Canterbury and Westland sides of the Main Divide in varying degrees of abundance. Liberations were made near Rotorua and at Waiho near the Franz Josef Glacier on the west coast of the South Island but neither was successful.

In contrast with the spread of chamois, another alpine dweller described in the previous chapter, the spread of thar has been relatively slow. During the sixty years since the initial liberation they have methodically worked north and south from their original point of release, but in much the same time chamois have colonised almost the entire mountain chain of the South Island. However, even today the spread of thar continues and there are periodic sightings of wandering individual animals or small groups far outside their known present range.

Although similar in appearance to large goats, thar are of much heavier build and a mature bull may weigh up to 300 pounds. Females weigh considerably less and seldom exceed 100 pounds. An impressive characteristic of a bull thar is its long body hair, which, around the neck and shoulders, forms an almost knee-length ruff or mane. Females do not have this mane and their body hair is much shorter. In males, the body hair varies from reddish to dark brown according to season and is generally much darker than that of females. Young animals are a more uniform greyish-brown, and kids are considerably lighter in colour than adults.

A unique feature of thar is the specialised hoof structure that enables them to negotiate sheer and dangerous rock faces with ease. Near-vertical bluffs which are apparently impassable to deer and even the nimble chamois present no barrier to thar. Nevertheless, accidents do occur and thar carcasses are sometimes found at the foot of cliffs and bluffs, presumably the outcome of misjudgments or avalanches. Mortality among juvenile thar is very high and this is probably due to prolonged periods of harsh weather at a stage of growth when their natural resistance is low.

Thar tend to remain in separate herds (of adult males, and immature animals and females) for the major part of the year. The mobs mix only for the rut, which generally takes place from late April to May or June. When mating is over the herds disperse into their separate groups again and the bulls move up to higher levels. Although thar normally inhabit the alpine grasslands and exposed crags far above the bush-line, with the onset of winter and during severe storms they often seek protection in the lower montane scrub belt. They are not generally found in high-altitude forests except during extremely adverse weather.

Where there are thar in concentrated numbers they have modified the vegetation of the area through their habit of selective feeding. Because of the preference for high-altitude pastures where available food is generally limited to species of alpine tussock and flowers, the survival of these plants has been endangered in many areas. In some catchments where thar herds have been resident for years unique and attractive flowers such as mountain daisies, mountain lilies, and mountain buttercups have been eliminated.

Protection of thar was lifted in 1930, but not until 1937 did official control operations against the animal begin. Since then more than 30,000 thar have fallen to Government hunters. Sportsmen have long regarded the thar as a specially desirable trophy, and many thousands have been taken by trophy hunters since protection was removed. Thar hunting is a young man's sport and because of the dangers associated with alpine hunting in rugged and treacherous country the hunter must have experience of climbing techniques and be properly equipped.

A herd of thar, two bulls and fifteen cows. On the ridge top above Carneys Creek, Rangitata River, Canterbury.

Thar country. Looking down Carneys Creek to Havelock Branch, Rangitata River, Canterbury.

RIGHT: Looking up the north branch of the upper Wilkin Valley, Otago, to Mt Pollux.

Lower Dart Valley in winter. The snow-covered peaks are Mt Nox and Mt Chaos.

Like chamois, thar inhabit the mountain tops of the Southern Alps. They are at home in this rugged country and severe climate. They seldom descend to lower altitudes. This picture shows a thar herd in its mountain home.

An example of destruction of alpine scrub by thar, which feed in groups, doing severe damage over a limited area.

Far above the realm of man, this bull thar displays the thick coat and neck ruff which enables him to withstand the harsh mountain climate.

FARM ANIMALS LIVING IN WILD STATE

L. H. Harris

FARM ANIMALS have escaped and lived in a wild state from the earliest times of European settlement in New Zealand. The subsequent development of livestock farming, especially the grazing of sheep and cattle over large individual holdings of rough and partly unfenced country, increased the opportunities for stock to stray. Later still the deterioration of some farms and eventually the abandonment of these holdings often led to animals, mainly cattle, becoming wild.

Rarely in New Zealand have farm animals been closely herded by an attendant as is still common in some countries. Even in the early stages of settlement stock, particularly sheep and cattle, roamed over rough, largely unfenced tracts cleared from the bush. Under these conditions cattle were not handled much and were very scary. They were made more so by boisterous droving during infrequent musters. When they did escape such animals quickly became truly wild.

In recent times better husbandry and the subdivision of holdings into manageable blocks have reduced the inclination of farm animals to stray far. Nevertheless in a few places there are still wild cattle, wild horses, and occasionally wild sheep.

In New Zealand neither cattle nor sheep that are wild yield trophy heads and there is little profit from carcases and hides or skins. Cattle that become permanent residents in native forest sometimes damage it severely; damage by sheep is less serious. Interbreeding between wild cattle and farm animals is sometimes a problem and has to be checked by hunting down wild bulls.

Horses were introduced by the early settlers about the beginning of the nineteenth century and since then animals have continually escaped or strayed. Showing a preference for isolated and thinly populated areas, horses have bred and existed in a semi-wild state. Herds, now limited mainly to the central North Island, particularly round Lake Taupo, have steadily declined over recent years. Their replacement rate seems to be slow and mortality high in the harsh winters of that area. Mountain barriers and large tracts of dense forest appear to have restricted their spread, and opportunity for increasing the size of herds has receded as more and more of the open land has been taken up and developed. The remaining small herds are rounded up periodically and the most promising animals broken-in and sold. Numbers have been drastically reduced by commercial operators supplying horsemeat to the flourishing pet food industry. Most people, however, are reluctant to shoot horses, which probably accounts for their relatively untouched, isolated existence over many years.

Cats and dogs belonging to the earliest European settlers must have escaped into the surrounding wilderness, because wild cats and dogs were reported as early as the 1820s. When rabbits (see page 130) began to increase alarmingly and seriously reduce the carrying capacity of farmland, cats were often liberated for control. Some settlers claimed that cats were highly effective in eliminating rabbits, but they are as likely to have destroyed large numbers of native and introduced birds and other wildlife. Today, fortunately, there are relatively few wild cats in forests, but they remain a threat to our native birds, many of which are not well adapted to evade them.

The long-extinct Maori dog or kuri did not live in the wild state, though it is believed that some dogs resulting from the interbreeding of Maori dogs and European introductions did become truly wild. There were many reports of packs of wild dogs doing serious damage to sheep flocks, in several parts of both islands during the latter half of the nineteenth century.

Packs of marauding dogs are still encountered in the central North Island back country and in the Urewera. Generally they are animals that have escaped from bush-edge farms or hunting parties. Their periodic sheep and calf-killing forays and the threat they pose to flightless birds are adequate reasons for destroying semi-wild dogs whenever they are encountered.

There have doubtless been many escapes of pigs and goats from farms. The occurrence of these animals in the wild state is discussed in separate sections.

WILD GOATS
L. H. Harris

THE GOATS *(Capra hircus)* found wild in New Zealand are descendants of liberated and escaped common domestic goats. Probably the first introduction was that made by Captain Cook, whose journals record the liberation in 1773 of a pair in a remote spot in Queen Charlotte Sound during Cook's second voyage to New Zealand. The spot was not remote enough to ensure their survival, for on his return to the same region during his last voyage in 1777 Cook discovered that the animals had fallen into the hands of Maoris and were dead. In making a gift of a further three goats (a male, female, and kid) he extracted a promise, in which he "put no great faith", that they should not be killed.

In all likelihood other early voyagers brought in goats. Often no doubt, the animals were bartered or given to Maoris. Some of the animals are certain to have gone wild before long, for in the early days the Maoris, who had no experience of animal husbandry, herded goats very loosely. Under prevailing conditions even the early European settlers would have found goats difficult to restrain, and escapers replenished and augmented the earliest wild herds.

There have since been many escapes of goats kept on farms, mainly for the control of blackberry — especially in Taranaki, Hawke's Bay, Nelson, and Marlborough.

During the latter half of the nineteenth century and well into the twentieth many deliberate liberations of goats were made on outlying islands to provide a source of food for castaways. About that time also acclimatisation societies introduced Angora goats, from which it was hoped would develop an industry using their fine wool. Angora goat herds reached sizeable proportions in the areas where they were introduced: Auckland, Canterbury, and Otago. However, interest in this venture faded and the neglected animals inevitably interbred with common goats. Even today some of the wild animals show characteristics of the Angora. Three Cashmere goats were introduced into Canterbury in 1867, but there is no record of what became of them.

On the two main islands of New Zealand the build-up of wild goat populations did not attract much attention until the 1930s. Marlborough and parts of Otago were the worst affected areas, the very high numbers providing serious competition for sheep for the available grazing. This, and the extent to which goats depleted almost all vegetation they could browse, led to the beginning of Government control operations in 1937.

In areas in which herds had grown unchecked Government hunters recorded very high tallies. The peak was in 1946, when 73,000 were shot. In 1950 bounties were introduced in several localities where goats were causing such widespread denudation of land that they were contributing to erosion.

Official control measures have accounted for over half a million goats, and the bounty and free ammunition schemes for a further 600,000. Sportsmen have also killed large numbers over many years.

Several control operations have been mounted against goat colonies on small outlying islands, on which their browsing has become damaging to vegetation and a threat to the existence of some plants. For example, in 1966 a team of Government hunters and wildlife scientists killed more than 3,000 goats on 764-acre Macauley Island in the Kermadec group, 600 miles northeast of New Zealand. Developing unchecked on isolated uninhabited islands previously free of grazing animals, goats have created havoc with protective vegetation.

Goats will eat the foliage of most trees and plants and can quickly destroy all vegetation within their reach; they are very nimble and have been seen to walk out on leaning tree trunks or branches to reach otherwise inaccessible foliage. In the forest they become extremely destructive; in places where they occur with deer the combined browsing and trampling tends to devastate vegetation.

As the illustrations show goats may vary con-

(continued on page 93)

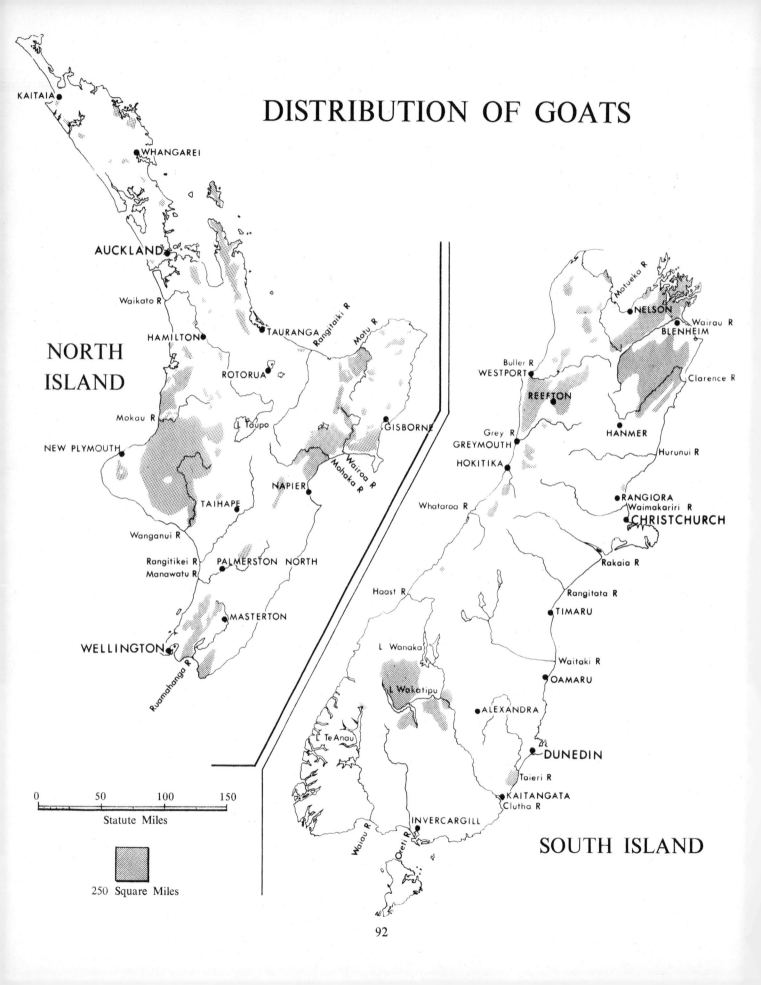

DISTRIBUTION OF GOATS

NORTH ISLAND

KAITAIA

WHANGAREI

AUCKLAND

Waikato R

HAMILTON

TAURANGA

Rangitaiki R

Motu R

ROTORUA

L Taupo

GISBORNE

Mokau R

NEW PLYMOUTH

Wairoa R

Mohaka R

NAPIER

TAIHAPE

Wanganui R

Rangitikei R

Manawatu R

PALMERSTON NORTH

MASTERTON

WELLINGTON

Ruamahanga R

SOUTH ISLAND

Motueka R

NELSON

Wairau R

BLENHEIM

Buller R

WESTPORT

Clarence R

REEFTON

Grey R

GREYMOUTH

HANMER

HOKITIKA

Hurunui R

Whataroa R

RANGIORA

Waimakariri R

CHRISTCHURCH

Rakaia R

Haast R

Rangitata R

TIMARU

L Wanaka

Waitaki R

OAMARU

L Wakatipu

ALEXANDRA

L Te Anau

DUNEDIN

Taieri R

KAITANGATA

Clutha R

Waiau R

INVERCARGILL

Oreti R

0   50   100   150

Statute Miles

250 Square Miles

92

This pair of playful goats was photographed in the Maungaharuru Range, Hawke's Bay.

siderably in size and colour. Plain whitish coats are common, though they may also be brown, black, and every conceivable combination of these, including speckled, spotted, and piebald. Male and female both have horns, but only those of the male achieve anything like trophy dimensions. A mature, thickly coated billy with heavy curling horns perhaps exceeding three feet in span is an impressive beast.

Hunters are usually reluctant to shoot goats, feeling that there is no sport or spirit of adventure in pursuing these inquisitive and often stupid creatures. The general lack of appeal of goat hunting as a sport means that in places their numbers will have to be kept down by Government control operations, probably for a long time to come.

A herd of wild goats in Hawke's Bay. If in high concentrations, goats can virtually eliminate the vegetation of an area through their sustained, non-selective browsing and their trampling.

RIGHT: An area of Mt Egmont attractive to goats, which find shelter under the bluffs. The alpine scrub has been completely stripped from the sector on the left of the picture by their browsing. Soil erosion is inevitable under the 200 in. rainfall of the locality.

In the Skippers Valley, Otago, goats, originally introduced by goldminers last century, became so plentiful that they affected the grazing available for domestic stock. Thousands of goats were shot in the locality in two successive winters immediately after the Second World War.

Goats kept by farmers for the control of blackberry have escaped and invaded many bush areas of Taranaki, including Egmont National Park. In recent years intensive control operations have done much to check the damage that was taking place.

WILD PIGS

L. H. Harris

CAPTAIN COOK liberated pigs *(Sus scrofa)* in New Zealand in 1773, and other introductions were made by voyagers after him. The origin and the species of these early liberations will always be shrouded in uncertainty, however, for the pigs released on our shores have progressively lost all evidence of their original characteristics through continual interbreeding with escaped domestic animals. The Maori's habit in the early days of raising and keeping his pigs in a semi-wild state led to frequent escapes into the bush, which replenished the wild herds and aided rapid spread through bush, bush margin, and scrub country.

It is safe to assume that the true wild pig was never introduced. The European wild boar is a large coarse-haired animal standing thirty-three to thirty-six inches at the shoulder. It often lacks the long bristles forming the pronounced dorsal crest (razor back) that distinguishes its close cousin, the Indian wild boar. The Hungarian and Russian wild pigs, because of their larger size, are yet another species. None of the descriptions of these animals tally with our own wild pig, which is almost certainly a result of interbreeding of several originally domestic types, including Tamworth, Hampshire, and Berkshire.

There is little information about the ecology of wild pigs in this country; and, despite the frequency with which they are hunted, no serious population studies have been made. Family groups are commonly seen, and populations appear to fluctuate markedly in any one locality. Mobs often travel considerable distances and in some places seem to be almost migratory. Damage they cause is generally confined to rooting, which modifies vegetation but seldom proves severe, except in pastures along bush edge areas containing substantial pig populations. Such pastures can take on the appearance of a ploughed field. Rooting in the bush on steep country can occasionally be sufficiently intense to start limited erosion. Another form of damage stems from the wild pigs' liking for new-born lambs, and losses can sometimes be heavy in areas where farmlands abut forest containing pigs. To cope with such situations, farmers often form groups to poison, shoot, and trap the pigs. In parts of the country a bounty is still paid for each pig killed.

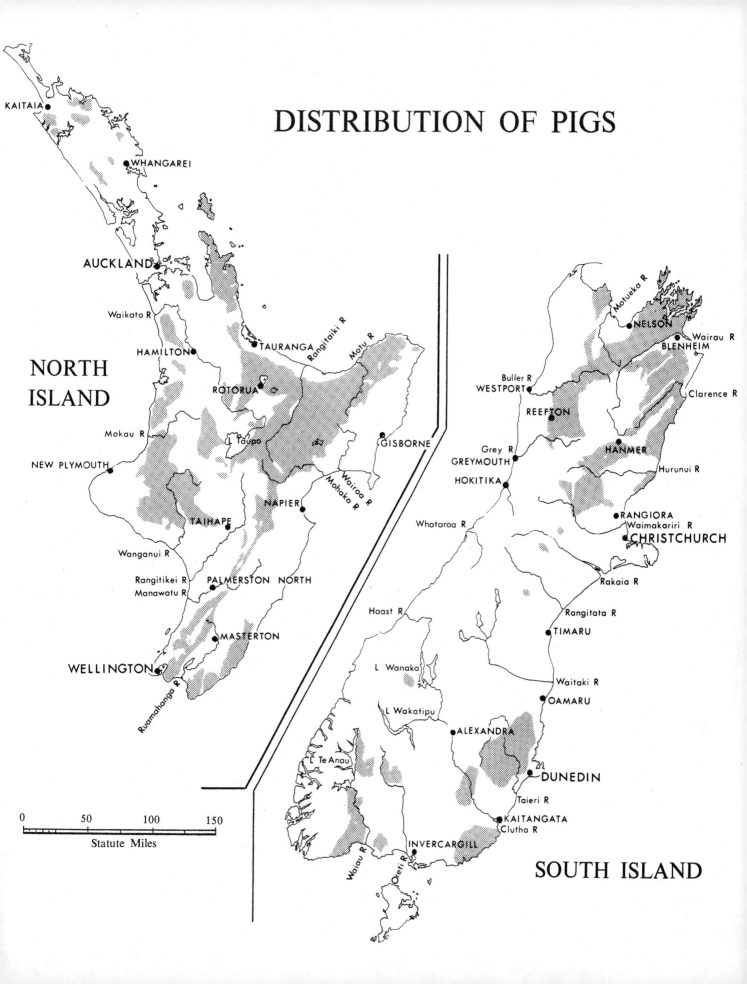

DISTRIBUTION OF PIGS

KAITAIA

WHANGAREI

AUCKLAND

NORTH
ISLAND

Waikato R

HAMILTON

TAURANGA

Rangitaiki R

Motu R

ROTORUA

Mokau R

L Taupo

GISBORNE

NEW PLYMOUTH

Wairoa R

Mohaka R

NAPIER

TAIHAPE

Wanganui R

Rangitikei R

Manawatu R

PALMERSTON NORTH

MASTERTON

WELLINGTON

Ruamahanga R

Motueka R

NELSON

Wairau R

BLENHEIM

Buller R

WESTPORT

Clarence R

REEFTON

Grey R

GREYMOUTH

HANMER

Hurunui R

HOKITIKA

Whataroa R

RANGIORA

Waimakariri R

CHRISTCHURCH

Rakaia R

Haast R

Rangitata R

L Wanaka

TIMARU

L Wakatipu

Waitaki R

OAMARU

ALEXANDRA

DUNEDIN

L Te Anau

Taieri R

KAITANGATA

Clutha R

Waiau R

INVERCARGILL

Oreti R

SOUTH ISLAND

0   50   100   150
Statute Miles

Pigs (and goats) were put ashore in New Zealand and some offshore islands by early explorers in expectation that they would multiply and provide a source of food for shipwrecked mariners.

Heavily built about the shoulders and neck with short, ungainly legs, wild pigs give the impression of being clumsy and slow-moving. To the contrary, even this large grey boar proved capable of surprising speed and agility when the camera shutter alarmed him.

Rolling country in which wallabies occur in the Hunter Hills, South Canterbury.

LEFT: Wild pigs in tussock grasslands at Lees Valley, Canterbury. Although found in many types of vegetation, they usually prefer the good concealment of bush and scrub.

Upper Travers River, Nelson Lakes National Park.

By rooting with their powerful snouts wild pigs do the damage shown. Wairau Valley, Marlborough.

MARSUPIALS
K. H. Miers

AMONG THE MAMMALS introduced into New Zealand is a group warranting special mention, the marsupials. All have come from Australia, which has about 230 species. Except for a small number of species in America, this group of primitive yet specialised mammals has died out elsewhere in the world; apparently they were not able to withstand the competition from more highly developed mammals.

Marsupials, which are furred, warm-blooded, and suckle their young, evolved into a variety of forms similar in appearance, habits, and environmental requirements to some of the higher mammals. For example, there are mouse-like and rat-like forms occupying habitats ranging from dense forests to deserts. The wallabies, wallaroos, and kangaroos comprise a large group of grazing animals filling a role similar to that of the antelope, deer, and cattle elsewhere in the world. In the forest there has evolved a variety of forms including the cuscus, koala, and opossum, some of which have the ability to glide from tree to tree. An interesting variety of cat-like and dog-like carnivorous marsupials also evolved.

It is in their reproduction that marsupials differ most markedly from the more highly evolved (placental) mammals. The embryos are born at a very early stage of development and crawl into a pouch or marsupium (fold or pocket of skin in the belly area), where development continues. In some marsupials the period between conception and birth may be as short as ten days; it is sixteen days for opossums and only thirty-three days for kangaroos.

Much popular fantasy has been indulged in over marsupial embryos and their manner of birth. Such biological absurdities as "they are born on the teat" are still heard. That the opossum, for example, has a gestation of only sixteen or seventeen days seems to be beyond the belief of many people. The tiny embryo is born and crawls through the fur to the marsupium, where it becomes attached to the teat.

The marsupials introduced into New Zealand, the opossum and six species of wallaby, are described in following sections.

OPOSSUMS

L. T. Pracy

THE BRUSHTAIL OPOSSUM *(Trichosurus vulpecula)*
a marsupial or pouched animal, is among the best-known of the introduced animals of New Zealand. It has wide distribution and, though nocturnal, is frequently seen because of its presence in trees and gardens in urban areas. Dead animals, killed by motor vehicles, are a common sight on roads.

There are eight subspecies of *T. vulpecula* that vary in size and colour; all are natives of Australia and neighbouring islands. In Australia they are protected, though snaring under licence is permitted periodically in some States. The first recorded successful liberation in New Zealand was that made in 1837-40 near Riverton, in Southland. Between then and 1898 at least thirty-eight further liberations were made of animals from the Australian mainland and Tasmania and another 360 known liberations from animals already acclimatised. The purpose of introductions was the establishment of a fur trade.

Most forests provided favourable habitats and establishment exceeded expectations; dispersal now is exceedingly wide and well beyond the confines of forests. Opossums, provided they can obtain palatable leaves, flowers, and fruits and can find suitable dry nest-sites in hollow logs and trees, will occupy various habitats, though the very heavy rainfall of Fiordland appears to deter full colonisation. The animals are to be found from the coasts to alpine scrublands. Population density depends on the habitat; if it provides good nesting sites and ample food, high populations may be attained.

The main breeding season is from April to May and normally only one young a year is born, though under favourable conditions where there is no overcrowding some animals breed twice a year.

Opossums are known to browse on many native trees or plants, but their preferred foods come from some of the species of small trees. Opossums do not thrive in the damp and cold conditions frequently found within native forests, but become established there if deer or other large animals open up the lower storey and thus induce drier conditions and improve access to food.

On farms and on urban land opossums are usually more of a nuisance than a serious threat. Locally they damage newly-sown pasture and fodder crops; fruit, shelter, timber, and ornamental trees; and vegetable and flower gardens. While searching for food they often break light branches and knock off twigs and fruit. Animals living on pastoral land may travel up to two miles at night to feed; in forests the feeding range is much shorter.

Trees in exotic forests may also be damaged, the extent depending on the vulnerability of species, the age of the trees, and the amount of cover available to opossums. If the damage warrants direct control measures, these are accepted as part of normal forest management.

The taking of opossum skins has been permitted since 1921 and has been carried on mainly by professional hunters in forest areas, who trap or poison the animals. Despite the recovery of large numbers of skins each season — over 1,000,000 in 1963 — commercial trapping and poisoning have done little to reduce populations and have not limited the spread of opossums. In 1951 a bounty for opossums killed was introduced in the hope that it would improve the measure of control given by hunting, but the scheme was ineffective and the bounty was eventually withdrawn in 1961.

Opossum control on pastoral lands has come progressively under the jurisdiction of pest destruction boards (formerly known as rabbit boards) or county councils. The Forest Service is responsible for control in all State forests and for control that protects pest destruction board areas from reinfestation from outside areas.

Despite the wide occurrence of opossums, the damage they do is only locally serious and does not warrant extensive regional control measures. Whether even local control will be justified needs to be determined by relating its cost to the improvement that is likely to be produced.

Now common in many districts, the opossum was introduced to establish a fur trade. This Australian marsupial quickly adapted to New Zealand conditions and is now a pest in some localities.

Forests containing southern rata (*Metrosideros umbellata*) and kamahi (*Weinmannia race-mosa*) are widespread on the steep western faces of the Southern Alps, where rainfall is 200–300 in. a year, possibly more. They have been invaded by red deer, which eat out the ground cover, and by opossums, which feed in the tree tops. The favourable conditions created by the deer below have led to the infestation of opossums becoming so heavy that many trees have died as a result of being stripped of leaves.

A southern rata killed by repeated complete defoliation as a result of opossum browsing.

WALLABIES
L. H. Harris

THE FAMILY to which wallabies belong also contains kangaroos, rat-kangaroos, and wallaroos. Wallabies and kangaroos were introduced into New Zealand from Australia during the late nineteenth century, but only the former survived.

Recent studies of wallabies in this country determined that six species have become naturalised. They are:

Red-necked or brush wallaby —
Macropus rufogrisea
Black-tailed or swamp wallaby —
M. bicolor
Black-striped wallaby —
M. dorsalis
Dama or tammar wallaby —
M. eugenii
White-throated or parma wallaby —
M. parma
Brush-tailed rock wallaby —
Petrogale penicillata

The largest and most extensive population is of the red-necked species in the Hunter Hills, behind Waimate, in South Canterbury. Here they have spread over an area of more than a million acres, though they are concentrated mainly in about a quarter of that area. This population is derived from three animals, one male and two females, liberated about 1874 purely as a curiosity. The habitat is predominantly tussock grassland, grazed by sheep, and has patches of bush and scrub in some gullies. The animals will thrive on ravaged country where the grazing is too poor for sheep farming. In addition, they are liable to damage all species of shrubs. The result is very severe reduction of vegetation in infested areas. Wallabies have also caused some damage to crops and young plantations of exotic trees.

In parts of the Hunter Hills the wallaby population was in excess of one animal an acre until control operations by the Wildlife Branch of the Department of Internal Affairs began in the winter of 1947. In the ensuing ten years Government hunters shot more than 68,000 wallabies in the area, mainly during winter because of other important commitments at other times. In 1959 the Rabbits Act was amended to allow rabbit boards to undertake wallaby control. Since then poisoning has been done regularly, with considerable success.

Wallabies are also to be found in the Rotorua region, where tammar wallabies were liberated about 1912. L. T. Pracy of the New Zealand Forest Service suspects that further releases were made about 1939, the animals being from Kawau Island near Auckland, where wallabies have been established for 100 years, having been introduced by a former owner of the island and Governor of New Zealand, Sir George Grey. Observations indicate that there is at least one species in addition to the tammar in the Rotorua area. In the early days increase in the district was slow, but now wallabies are found east and north of Lake Rotorua to Lake Rerewhakaaitu and the northern boundary of Kaingaroa State Forest.

In this area wallabies generally inhabit undeveloped areas of native grass, scrub, and fern and to a limited extent cut-over logged indigenous forest. Browsing damage to forests and grassland around Rotorua is generally negligible, but there has been locally serious destruction of crops near the edges of forest and scrub. Intermittent poisoning and shooting by rabbit boards continues in the worst affected areas.

Of the six species of wallaby successfully liberated in New Zealand, four and perhaps five may still exist on a number of islands in the Hauraki Gulf in varying degrees of abundance. They are the tammar wallaby, parma wallaby, black-tailed wallaby, and black-striped wallaby (all on Kawau Island) and the brush-tailed rock wallaby (on Kawau, Rangitoto, and Motutapu Islands).

The black-striped wallaby is certainly very rare on Kawau if not extinct. Wallaby numbers have been reduced periodically on the islands to prevent excessive damage to vegetation. The parma wallaby, which is considered nearly extinct in its native Australia, was only very recently identified on Kawau. Specimens have already been sent to Australia in an effort to re-establish the species in its homeland.

The parma or white-throated wallaby is found only on Kawau Island in the Hauraki Gulf, near Auckland. Reports suggest that the parma is extremely rare, possibly close to extinction, in its native Australia.

In addition to occurring on a few islands in the Hauraki Gulf, wallabies exist in the Hunter Hills (South Canterbury) and round Rotorua, where this dama or tammar wallaby was photographed.

LEFT: Haunts of the dama wallaby on hill country bordering Lake Tarawera.

115

A red-necked or brush wallaby of the Hunter Hills.

LEFT: Modified tussock grassland on the Hunter Hills, Canterbury, where the red-necked or brush wallaby is found, spread over about a million acres of similar country. Numbers are so high that there is not enough grazing for domestic stock. Although thousands of animals have been shot, this form of control was found only partially effective and has been replaced by poisoning, undertaken by local pest destruction boards.

117

HARES

J. E. C. Flux

HARES (*Lepus europaeus*) were introduced into New Zealand from Britain for sport. The first to arrive are said to have jumped into the sea through a porthole when their ship, the *Eagle*, docked in Lyttelton in 1851. They managed to swim ashore and established themselves on the Port Hills. In the following twenty years several importations were made from both Britain and Australia, and by the 1880s hares were so plentiful in parts of Canterbury that shooting restrictions were lifted. They are now common in practically all suitable areas in both North and South Islands, but have not been introduced on to Stewart Island or any of the offshore islands.

The natural range of these hares extends from Britain to central Russia and from Finland to Israel. They have been introduced successfully into Siberia, Sweden, Ireland, eastern Canada and the USA, the Bahamas, South America, and Australia. Hares live on open grassland which has some scrub available for cover, and in New Zealand occur from sea level to alpine grassland at 6,000 feet.

Hares can be distinguished from their smaller relative, the rabbit, by their richer tawny colour, black-tipped ears, and characteristic loping run in the open when disturbed; rabbits scuttle to the nearest cover or burrow. The main zoological difference is that young hares are born fully furred with their eyes open, while young rabbits are blind and far less developed at birth. Hares are mainly nocturnal, spending the day in a grassy "form", which may be in the open or concealed below a bush or tussock. They are more solitary than rabbits, although groups of up to a dozen may be seen fighting and chasing in spring.

Breeding extends from July to April, with over 90 per cent of the females pregnant from August to February. The timing of the breeding season is almost entirely controlled by day length and breeding starts two to four weeks after the shortest day in all countries. Litter size varies seasonally in New Zealand, as overseas, with a small first litter of one, followed by litters of two to three later. Litters of more than five are unusual. The gestation period is six weeks and each female may have four or five litters a year, producing a total of about ten young. Young hares weigh three and a half to five and a half ounces at birth and grow to full size (seven and a half pounds for males, eight and a half pounds for females) in about five months. Females born early in the spring can start breeding later in the same season in New Zealand although this seldom happens in Europe.

Hares are entirely vegetarian and eat grasses and clover on agricultural land, and blue and snow tussock in alpine areas. In New Zealand they are regarded primarily as pests because they compete with domestic stock for grazing and damage young trees. They are not favoured as food or for sport, although winter hare drives are popular in parts of the South Island, and hunt clubs chase them with hounds. Pest destruction boards shoot many at night by spotlighting from Landrovers, but control on rough country is difficult because hares do not take bait readily. Unlike rabbits, hares have not been decommercialised and in 1965-66 the value of hares exported from New Zealand exceeded $140,000. Overseas they are highly esteemed as game and in Europe more than five million are shot each year by sportsmen.

A hare photographed on the Avoca River flats, Canterbury. Larger size and longer legs and ears distinguish the hare from its close relative the rabbit.

Modified tussock grassland at the confluence of the Harper and Avoca Rivers, Canterbury.
Hares are plentiful throughout this type of country and compete with sheep for the grazing.

RIGHT: Hares also wantonly damage young trees. The top of this Douglas fir has been nipped
off; but not eaten.

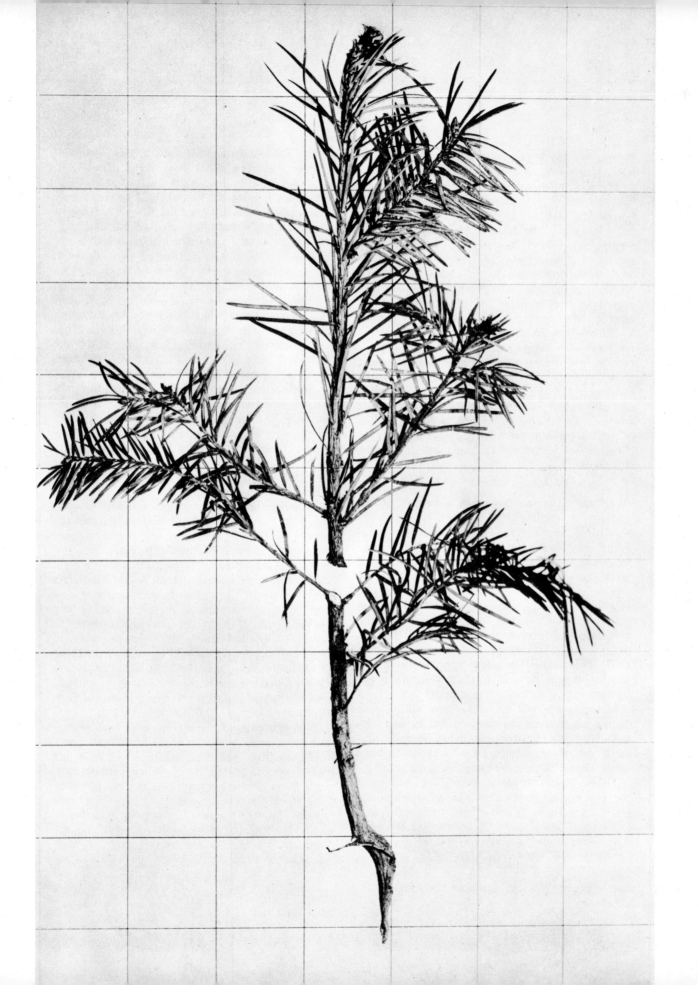

SMALL MAMMALS
L. H. Harris

WHEN THE FIRST EUROPEANS reached New Zealand, there existed only four species of land-dwelling mammals. These were two species of bat, the native rat (kiore), and the Maori dog (kuri). The last two animals are certain to have been introduced by Maori colonisers; the bats, therefore, have the distinction of being the only species of mammal truly indigenous to New Zealand. With such a paucity of animal life it was no wonder that the early European settlers displayed such enthusiasm for introductions. It is recorded that in the years soon after settlement began bandicoots, hedgehogs, racoons, stoats, ferrets, weasels, chipmunks, squirrels, guinea pigs, rabbits, and hares were imported and released without thought of possible consequences. Fortunately, some of the liberations failed and eventually only rabbits, hares, hedgehogs, ferrets, stoats, and weasels became sufficiently well established to earn a place in this book.

Hares and rabbits are discussed separately elsewhere.

MUSTELIDS: The family to which weasels, stoats, and ferrets belong (Mustelidae) is of almost worldwide distribution. Ferrets were first introduced into New Zealand in 1867 and during the following thirty years many liberations of all three species of mustelids were made both by private individuals and Government agencies in an effort to control rabbits after they had reached pest proportions. In fact, large-scale importation, breeding, and liberation of ferrets by the Department of Agriculture continued until about 1897. There has been some speculation that a number of true polecats were also imported, but nothing has come to light to support this.

Most laymen will probably have difficulty in distinguishing between weasels, stoats, and ferrets. However, except perhaps in juvenile animals, the three species have physical features which enable them to be identified quite readily.

The weasel *(Mustela nivalis)* is the smallest of the group, seldom exceeding a total length of nine inches. Its fur is brown with light underparts and its tail is short, wholly brown, and tapering. The white underparts of the weasel are often lightly spotted with brown.

The stoat or ermine *(Mustela erminea)* is about thirteen to fifteen inches long, with a dark brown coat and whitish underparts. A feature that distinguishes it from the weasel is its comparatively longer, bushy, black-tipped tail. In winter the coat may turn white, especially in the South Island.

The common ferret *(Mustela putorius)* is the largest of the mustelids found in New Zealand, adults having an overall length of from nineteen to twenty-four inches. The animal has a creamy, woolly undercoat with an overlay of longer, black-tipped hairs which gives a general darkish appearance. The legs and slightly bushy tail are usually somewhat darker than the rest of the body and there is a brown band across the face, including the area round the eyes.

All three species are widely distributed throughout New Zealand in varying degrees of abundance, but there are areas where one or more of the species now seem to be absent. For instance, the greater portion of Taranaki appears to be free of ferrets, and weasels do not appear to occur in several large areas in the South Island.

Whether or not mustelids actually assisted much in the control of rabbits, which was the reason for their introduction, will probably never be satisfactorily confirmed. The fact remains, however, that where rabbit populations were high, stoats and ferrets appeared to be abundant. As rabbit-control operations gained impetus and populations were reduced to low levels, so did the numbers of mustelids decline. It therefore seems likely that mustelids were probably in large part dependent on rabbits rather than being effective in controlling them. It has been widely believed that mustelids create havoc among native birdlife, but it is difficult to get evidence of such depredations.

Stomach samples have indicated that mustelids have eaten birds, domestic fowls (and eggs), and even frogs, but the greater part of their diet would appear to consist of young rabbits, rats, and mice. There seems little doubt, however, that if rabbits are absent, such as within indigenous forests, stoats and weasels, because of their climbing ability, do prey on birds and rob nests. How serious is the overall effect on birdlife is not at all clear.

The common ferret was introduced into New Zealand to control rabbits.

HEDGEHOG: Hedgehogs (*Erinaceus europaeus*) were imported into New Zealand during the latter stages of a period of sustained activity in the introduction of animals. The first of the species were released in the South Island in 1870, but until about the turn of the century the North Island was devoid of these animals. Hence, hedgehogs are relatively new "settlers".

Originally introduced to control insects such as snails in home gardens, hedgehogs are now widely spread throughout both islands. They are to be found mainly in gardens, orchards, hedgerows, and paddocks at relatively low altitude. Forest areas containing dense bush and alpine country are usually free of hedgehogs, conditions there presumably being unsuitable for them. There has not been an accurate assessment of present distribution and density of hedgehogs. It would be a difficult task because the animals, being nocturnal, may be in an area for a considerable time before being sighted. Observation is further complicated by the hedgehog's habit of hibernating for varying periods during harsh winter months. There is sufficient evidence, however, to indicate that hedgehogs on both islands are increasing and gradually extending their range.

Although small, seldom exceeding 9 in. long, the weasel is a fearless fighter. It has been observed raiding nests of native birds when ground prey such as rabbits, rats, and mice are scarce.

In the absence of a detailed scientific survey, how useful or harmful hedgehogs may be remains the subject of controversy. One faction, consisting mainly of gardeners and orchardists, considers hedgehogs to be beneficial because they eat beetles, grubs, slugs, woodlice, and snails. On the other hand, the animals are also claimed to eat the eggs of quail, duck, pheasant, and chukor and to kill young birds. There appears to be evidence to support these accusations in areas where there are a large number of hedgehogs, but guilt is not fully proved.

RAT: Rats hold a unique position in the collection of animals presented in this book, because in the wild state they possess absolutely no qualities beneficial to mankind. They are carriers of animal and human diseases and are a constant threat to agricultural produce, property, and general well-being. They have no friends or admirers.

At least three species of rat have become established in New Zealand. The earliest immigrant, the native rat or kiore *(Rattus exulans)* is believed to have been brought from Polynesia by the

Although similar in appearance to the weasel the stoat is about twice as big and its tail is longer, more bushy and has a black tip. In very cold countries the stoat assumes a white winter coat which provides the fur known as ermine.

early Maori settlers. The animal was a prized food of the Maoris, but was very rare even before the end of last century. Apart from a few specimens in captivity, the native rat may now be considered extinct on the main islands of New Zealand. It thrives on certain offshore islands.

The other two species, the "ship" or "roof" rat *(Rattus rattus)* and brown or Norwegian rat *(Rattus norvegicus)*, undoubtedly came with the early European explorers. Rats seem to have been permanent residents of sailing ships and it is logical to assume that there were often occasions when they were able to get ashore.

Inevitably, because of their adaptability, hardiness, and fecundity they spread quickly throughout New Zealand and also became abundant in numerous offshore islands.

Although ship rats are often found in warehouses, docks, etc., they are also common in rural and forest habitats. Norwegian rats, on the other hand, are essentially urban dwellers, preferring to live in burrows, often near water.

MOUSE: The grey-brown European house mouse *(Mus musculus)* is common in New Zealand, not only in buildings but outdoors, even living in

Hedgehog.

Native or Maori rat (kiore).

high country up to 4,000 feet. There have been mice in this country at least since the early 1830s, when they were reported in the Bay of Islands.

Mice seen in grassland or field crops are often referred to as field mice, but all, wherever they live, are of the one species.

Mice have become a pest in exotic forests because of the large amount of fallen tree seed they eat. This reduces the regrowth on harvested areas. They are equally destructive when seed is actually sown, and large-scale poisoning has been done to control mice on areas where trees are being established by seeding.

NEW ZEALAND BAT: But for the occurrence of two species of bat New Zealand would be a country without a single truly indigenous mammal. New Zealand species are the short-tailed bat *(Mystacina tuberculata)* and the long-tailed *(Chalinolobus tuberculatus)*. Neither species, though occurring throughout New Zealand, is often seen. They are primarily forest dwellers, inhabiting hollow trees and occasionally limestone caves. Though they were fairly common last century, reduction of forest areas since then seems to have decreased their distribution. New Zealand bats have failed to colonise open country or to adapt themselves to urban areas.

The long-tailed bat is closely related to Australian and South African types, but the short-tailed bat belongs to a genus found only in New Zealand. There are two distinct forms: One is found throughout the North Island and portions of Nelson and Marlborough. Another larger form has been recorded only on Stewart Island and neighbouring islets. Nowhere are bats prolific, though there are well-established colonies in the Urewera and Waikaremoana districts, upper Wanganui, Nelson, north-west Marlborough, and northern Westland. The highest densities of bats are probably in the Urewera forest in the North Island and the Buller River catchment in the South Island.

Bats navigate at night by an extremely complex and efficient "sonar" (echo location) system. While the animal is flying above a forest or along a bush fringe the sonar pulses are transmitted slowly (about five per second). The rate increases to about 200 per second when the bat gets a "fix" on a flying insect and begins to "home in". The range of transmission of these sonar pulses can generally extend over distances from a few inches up to about 100 feet: thus vision is not important during the animal's night-time wanderings.

A short-tailed bat from Mutton Bird Islands, Foveaux Strait. The presence of two species of bats saves New Zealand from being a country without truly native land animals. The so-called native dog (now extinct) and native rat (now rare on the main islands) were introduced from Polynesia by the Maoris about, it is thought, 600 years ago.

BELOW: The head of a short-tailed bat; its ears are long whereas those of the other native species, the long-tailed bat, are short. ABOVE: Wings extended.

New Zealand's short-tailed bat is the only species in the world that can crawl and climb with agility.

RABBITS

K. H. Miers

THOUGH THERE were many liberations of European rabbits *(Oryctolagus cuniculus)* in both the North and South Islands from the earliest stages of organised European settlement, they do not appear to have become firmly established in the wild until the 1860s. The first really successful liberation seems to have been in the sandhills near Invercargill in 1862.

As early as 1869 rabbits were reported as a nuisance in Southland and Marlborough, and in Central Otago by 1878. Most of the South Island country favourable to rabbits is likely to have been infested by the 1880s.

In the North Island the spread of rabbits was slower, presumably because of less favourable conditions (wetter climate, large forested areas, fewer extensive open tracts, and a different pattern of land development). Rabbits are said to have appeared in the Wairarapa about 1863; but not until the 1900s do they seem to have been numerous and widely dispersed.

For New Zealand as a whole rabbits are considered to have become most numerous just after the Second World War. By that time they had occupied all areas that suited them.

The harmful effects of rabbits on grassland devoted to livestock grazing prompted attempts at control as early as 1876. For many years there was reliance on a combination of methods that included the trapping of rabbits for carcasses and skins, poisoning with recovery of skins, destruction without recovery, and rabbit-proofing of properties by the erection of wire netting fences sunk in the ground.

Hopes of controlling rabbits by so-called natural enemies led to numerous liberations of weasels, stoats, ferrets, and cats by Government officers and others from about 1882 to 1890. Such liberations were often strenuously, though unsuccessfully, opposed on the grounds that the predators could be equally dangerous to useful small animals or birds, especially flightless native species. Over the years there have been conflicting claims on local effectiveness of predators, but there is no evidence that they ever reduced the overall rabbit population significantly. Stoats and ferrets are now very widely distributed, some of the areas in which the former occur being quite remote from any rabbits.

Increasing concern about rabbit damage and the loss of farm income attributed to it eventually led (in 1947) to the introduction of measures to co-ordinate rabbit destruction. Numbers have since been reduced spectacularly, mainly through aerial spreading of poison baits, supported by intensive hunting.

Rabbits thrive on light, well-drained soils where there is a combination of abundant cover and open ground on which close-cropped turf can be maintained. The animals dislike extensive areas of long grass, and populations may decline when pasture growth exceeds their ability to keep swards short.

Habitat favouring rabbits has already been greatly disturbed by closer settlement, more intensive development of farms, and by the subdivision of large holdings. These trends seem certain to continue, so that surroundings for wild rabbits can be expected to become progressively less favourable.

Rabbits never penetrated far into native forests, though at the time of their rapid dispersal in Southland they reached the forests of the western fiords. Though much of this movement would have been via the open tops, considerable travelling through forest would probably have been necessary and the animals are likely to have had to find subsistence there in winter.

In exotic forests rabbits may eat the foliage of newly planted trees, though they do no damage after the foliage has grown beyond their reach. In some areas control operations may have to be undertaken periodically as part of the regional eradication measures to forestall any resurgence, which under favourable conditions could occur very quickly.

RIGHT: A source of children's affection in fable and film the world over, the wild rabbit in New Zealand quickly became a serious pest of farmlands.

A painting by John Ferneley (1782–1860), a leading British animal painter of his time (by courtesy of T. R. Giles). Game was once a major source of meat in Great Britain, whence the present red deer population of New Zealand was derived.

COMMERCIAL ASPECTS OF
WILD ANIMALS
P . C . Logan

OF ALL THE ANIMALS introduced and allowed to live in a wild state rabbits, hares, opossums, deer, pigs, and goats have been most sought after for truly commercial purposes. Only the opossum was brought in deliberately for a specific commercial purpose: to provide a fur industry. The others were introduced to supply food and sport for the settlers, who missed the game animals of their homelands.

RABBIT: An export trade in rabbit skins began in the 1870s, less than ten years after the animal became established in the wild. In 1893 over 17 million skins were exported, a total not exceeded until 1924, when over 20 million were exported. Totals in later years often exceeded 10 million, but were falling (as a result of better land management and direct control measures) before commercial exploitation of rabbits was prohibited in 1957 as part of the campaign to eradicate them.

Overseas markets for rabbit carcasses did not open up until refrigerated ships became available after 1882. However by 1900 exports of frozen rabbits (in skins) had reached 6,500,000. Thereafter exports of carcasses (in skins and separate) declined until a revival during the economic depression of the early 1930s. Subsequently exports remained above one million carcases a year until the trade was interrupted by the Second World War. Exports ceased when commercial exploitation of rabbits was halted as part of the campaign to eliminate rabbits. As with many pest animals the cost of control and the losses in farm revenue were far higher than had been yielded by the sale of carcasses and skins.

HARE: Exports of hare skins and carcasses were recorded separately up to 1935, after which they were included with figures for rabbits. Probably not more than 50,000 carcasses and skins were ever exported in one year. Hares are killed during rabbit board control operations, but not until

1959 were boards given powers to control hares in the same way as rabbits. However, hare carcasses can still be exported.

OPOSSUM: After their introduction opossums were protected to permit them to build up numbers. Even so a trade in opossum skins, including exports, began long before trapping became legal. One report claims that in 1912 60,000 skins were taken in the Catlins district, Southland, alone. When the taking of skins under licence began in 1921 the total officially recorded was 25,180. Up to one million skins a year have since been exported, and total returns have exceeded $2 million (in 1970). Since 1947 there have been no restrictions on the taking of opossums.

DEER: Until 1930 herds had a degree of protection. There had been an attempt to sell deer meat in 1919, but at first the main commercial interest was in skins. Exports have fluctuated with the prices offering for these, reaching a peak in 1945-47, and in 1946 were worth $300,000, but have always been handicapped by price irregularities.

The export of venison, which began in 1952, has built up over the last ten years to a substantial, highly organised trade. In 1971 its earnings were $4.7 million for meat and $382,000 for skins. Returns are expected to decline because of heavy exploitation of areas where deer have been numerous.

WILD PIG AND GOAT: Wild pigs were not exploited commercially, except for local sales of meat to hotels, until a market for wild pork developed in conjunction with game meat exports about 1959. Wild pig numbers are not high and are possibly declining. Nevertheless about $300,000 dollars a year has been earned from exports.

An export trade in goat skins and meat began about 1942, when wild goat numbers were prob-

133

ably the highest they have ever been and Government assistance was given in the establishment of markets. Now hides and processed carcasses to the value of about $200,000 a year are exported.

OTHER TRADE: There has been a small export of live wallabies since 1966. Small quantities of chamois and thar meat and hides are taken by venison exporters.

HUNTING: Hunting trips can be arranged through professional guides who can book accommodation and provide special transport. Worldwide air travel and services within New Zealand are making shooting areas increasingly accessible, but actual hunting is often over rugged terrain, demanding agility and endurance.

Trade in deerskins was very prosperous for about ten years from 1940. Their collection attracted a number of colourful characters. The pictures show Ted Porter, Cliff Thomson, and the late Joff Thomson packing out skins to the collecting point, where they were transferred to packhorses. In one enterprise a Bren gun carrier was used.

Where red deer are very plentiful on the open mountain tops the difficulties of access to obtain venison for export have been overcome by using helicopters. Sometimes the hunters are landed, sometimes the helicopter is used as a shooting platform. Carcases are also lifted out to the roadhead by helicopter. This type of operation was used first in the rugged country of South Westland and western Otago, where herds of red deer were dense. It has since been employed elsewhere, sometimes in conjunction with Forest Service control operations.

Hunting, though physically demanding in New Zealand, is enjoyed by many. Here a well-known American sportsman and writer on the outdoors, Warren Page, is approaching a trophy red deer stag in the Dart Valley, Otago.

FOR TOURISTS AND HUNTERS
L. H. Harris

INFORMATION ABOUT MOUNTAIN and forest recreation areas, wildlife, fishing waters, field facilities, etc. can be obtained from a number of sources. Almost every major town has a Forest Service officer, national park ranger, wildlife ranger (of the Department of Internal Affairs), acclimatisation society, or some fishing, hunting, or tramping club able to assist visitors.

When visiting forested areas people are cautioned to take special care with fires and cigarettes at all times, particularly during the fire-risk season from October to April. Carelessness can cause untold damage to thousands of acres of forest valuable for timber, for bird and animal

shelter, and for protective cover to the soil. Camp fires must be carefully sited where they will not spread to vegetation and must be completely extinguished when the party leaves. Visitors are expected to keep sites free of litter and not to disturb unnecessarily plant growth or surroundings.

All wildlife in New Zealand (bird, fish, and animal) is the property of the State until lawfully captured or killed, and then ownership automatically transfers to the hunter or fisherman. With the exception of fresh-water game fish, water fowl, upland game birds, protected birds, and wapiti, all wildlife may be hunted at any time,

138

without licence, monetary fee, or bag limit. The only restriction is that permission must be obtained from the controlling authority ·or land-owner where the game is to be sought. On the vast areas of Crown lands this is obtained from the Department of Lands and Survey, the New Zealand Forest Service, or a particular national park board. Access to private lands is a matter of negotiation between the sportsman and the landowner or lessee. It is a point of courtesy as well as a legal obligation to obtain permission to enter any land for any purpose. Only in national parks and state forest parks is entry unrestricted, and then only *without a firearm*.

Taking of game birds and game fish is regulated by licensing that specifies the seasons for them, bag limits, methods, and other conditions. Licences are available from most sports goods stores or, in country districts, from post offices and general stores. Usually the season begins about 1 May for water fowl and 1 October for trout.

Though a licence is not required to hunt wapiti, conditions are imposed by the Fiordland National Park Board, which regulates entry into the park with a firearm.

Rabbits and hares may be killed without a licence at any time, except where a pest destruc-tion board operation is in progress. Permission to enter on to land is the only requirement.

In national parks and similar reserves *all bird life* is protected.

Ownership of firearms in New Zealand is strictly controlled by the police, and readers are advised to apply to the police for details. Briefly the present main requirements for ownership are:
- Age at least sixteen years. `
- If between sixteen and twenty, parental consent is necessary.
- A permit to procure a firearm must be obtained from the police, then
- The firearm must be taken to police for registration.
- Overseas visitors must register firearms on arrival.

Low-power rim-fire rifles such as .22 calibre are not permitted in national parks and in state forests they are permitted only in exceptional circumstances, because of their threat to bird life and inadequacy on big game. Similarly, only under special circumstances and with express permission are shotguns allowed in these areas.

Wherever the hunter may be, there is always the possibility of others being in the vicinity, and for this reason he must be extremely care-ful and identify his target beyond all possible doubt before firing.

DEER FARMING AND DEER PARKS
P. C. Logan

ESTABLISHMENT OF DEER FARMING, still very much in its infancy in New Zealand, is seen as a means of maintaining an export trade in venison. At present this is based on extensive hunting of wild animals, including use of helicopters for reach-ing hunting areas and recovery of carcases. It is realised that these expensive operations will be-come uneconomic when large numbers of deer can no longer be recovered regularly.

The game meat industry is anxious to preserve the trade to protect its investment in processing plant. Venison exports were valued at $4.7 million in 1971.

To permit deer farming it was necessary to amend legislation relating to deer control; this was done after an investigation by a parliamen-tary select committee, which reported in favour of deer farming subject to certain safeguards.

The amending legislation stipulates that deer species may not be held and bred from in any area which is outside the known range of wild deer of that species. This removes the possibility of escaping animals forming the nucleus of herds in areas previously free of deer or of particular species. A permit to farm deer may be refused if land is likely to erode as a consequence of its use as a deer farm; or if effective deer-proof fences cannot or will not be erected and main-tained; or if the Director-General of Agriculture considers that animal health and disease preven-tion may be endangered. The legislation also en-sures that farmed deer are not to be regarded as noxious animals and cannot be hunted or killed as wild deer. However, a deer that escapes may be killed as a noxious animal unless it is branded or otherwise identified as a farmed animal.

There is no information on the economics and

Recent legislation has permitted the establishment of deer farms, subject to the observance of strict requirements. This farm near Lake Taupo, developed by Consolidated Traders Ltd., was the first established for commercial purposes.

practical problems of holding, breeding, and raising deer for slaughter and production of venison for export. All the problems of conventional, cattle or sheep raising, plus new problems, will no doubt have to be overcome. When domesticated deer are comparatively easy to rear but once tamed they lose all fear of human beings and can be dangerous. The movement and handling of large numbers of deer for veterinary inspection is likely to be difficult.

Nevertheless, farm-bred venison under veterinary inspection will be accepted into countries which now bar imported venison killed in the wild. Moreover the meat might well command a higher price than does game meat, the average for which is 35 cents a pound. On the other hand fencing costs are higher than for conven-

tional cattle fences, deer farm stock cannot be bought readily, and the cost of establishing and stocking a deer farm will be high. If the nucleus stock are to be captured from the wild, the prospective deer farmer may also have to compete with commercial and private hunters at any time. Suitable land will not be easy to get, especially land which can be expected to sustain high stocking and quick weight gain. It is fortunate that Lincoln College, University of Canterbury, has decided to undertake study of the practical problems and economics of farming red deer.

Deer Parks

Deer parks, in which deer are held for public exhibition and as a tourist attraction, will compete with deer farms for available animals. Some

140

This fine, park-reared stag appears very tame, but when the rutting (mating) season begins he will lose all fear of man and become belligerent and potentially dangerous.

Hind and calf in a deer park. Such parks are being established as an attraction for tourists and holidaymakers.

deer parks will be purely local attractions, established to meet a need for another civic attraction; a few will be on the main tourist routes. A smaller number still are expected to be licensed as class B zoological gardens and to hold other introduced animals and perhaps native birds. Private persons will be allowed to hold and breed deer in areas in which the species to be held already occurs wild; but if breeding in captivity is not possible, they may be permitted to hold any species.

Deer parks or class B zoological gardens administered by a city council or board of trustees may be allowed to hold breeding stock of several species under very strict conditions. An important condition is that the enclosure must at all times be under the supervision of a resident caretaker.

Although there has been relaxation of the law regarding the keeping of deer in captivity, there are safeguards to preclude the possibility of land or vegetation being degraded. The liberation of deer species into previously deer-free areas is also guarded against, and heavy penalties are prescribed for breaches.

There have already been (June 1972) 88 applications for permits to establish deer farms and deer parks.

143

PHOTOGRAPHIC NOTES
J. H. Johns

THE ANIMAL PHOTOGRAPHS in this book were taken primarily to show the physical characteristics of their subjects. In the limited time available, it was not possible to record for each animal a complete range of wild life studies, but this was attempted wherever possible.

EQUIPMENT: Before a camera to cover this project was selected considerable thought had to be given to the main uses of the results from all the field assignments. In addition to use in this book the photographs were required for permanent record and exhibition. Although the 35 mm format is excellent for recording individual animals, a larger negative is desirable to show groups of animals, forest, and land forms. A few of the photographs were taken on 4in x 5in and 35 mm cameras, but most of them were taken on a Hasselblad camera (2¼in x 2¼in format) using 60 mm, 80 mm, 150 mm, 250 mm, and 500 mm lenses and interchangeable film magazines.

TRIPODS: To obtain the best results from a precision camera, camera shake must be eliminated; therefore nearly all the photographs were taken using a sturdy 4 lb tripod. The most suitable model proved to be a modified wooden theodolite tripod. Heavy duty equipment is technically desirable for the best results, but the extra weight and bulk would be prohibitive for operating in the mountains and back country.

A shoulder-stock camera support is useful for close stalking when a rock or tree can be used for support and lighting conditions are suitable. But this method is not reliable for eliminating camera shake.

The fallow deer herd was the only photograph taken from a tree hide. Hides were tried on other occasions, but stalking was by far the most effective method of getting close to the animals.

FILM: The highest film speed possible is required to photograph wild animals. Tests in black and white on domestic animals indicated that for subjects in sunlight F.P.3 used at 200 Weston would produce very good quality prints. For subjects in poor or dull light F.P.3 used at 400 Weston gave the best combination of speed and fine grain. Microphen was selected for the film developer. For various reasons, priority was given to monochrome black and white recording. Only a small number of animals were photographed on colour film. For this, Ektachrome Professional and Ektacolour Professional were used. Preference was later given to colour negative film because it provided both colour prints and transparencies.

FLASHLIGHT: Two rusa deer were photographed at night at a range of sixteen yards (see page 42) using a 250 mm lens and two flash guns fitted with P.F.100 bulbs fired simultaneously. Quick camera focussing proved very difficult, even when assisted by a companion with a powerful spotlight.

CAMOUFLAGE: Complete camouflage of photographer, camera, and tripod is important to obtain more than one photograph of an animal when using a tripod and also a camera which is not silent in operation. This was proved when photographing the whitetail buck and chamois at approximately seventeen yards and also the sika stag at twenty-four yards, when four photographs were taken.

Camouflage consisted of an army head net and similar nets to cover camera equipment. Green woollen mittens made from socks and an olive green woollen swandri proved to be the best body cover — the colour was more effective than an army camouflage jacket and it made less noise when the photographer was moving through scrub. In hot weather a lightweight green and red-flecked woollen shirt was used. This blended with most vegetation and especially well with manuka.

All the animals were difficult to photograph, red deer being the most accommodating, and sambar the most difficult. In one instance a sambar stag and hind were caught. This operation proved less difficult than photographing these animals.

A small number of whitetail deer found in the Lake Wakatipu district took several days of stalking before being recorded. It was relatively simple to get within seventy yards of them, but they were most frustrating to photograph at a range of sixteen to thirty yards.

Camouflaged photographer.

Competition with hunters was a major problem. Undisturbed areas were difficult to find and in most of the animal assignments particular attention was paid to information provided by local residents and local forest rangers. Fiordland proved to be a formidable region with its combination of wet weather and rugged terrain. The weather made it necessary to record the wapiti bull from 170 yards, which is out of camera range. However, a chance exposure was made, as this was likely to be the last opportunity of photographing a good bull.

A few of the animals were photographed in captivity, as it was found impossible to find time to photograph them in the wild.

TYPICAL ANTLER FORMATIONS

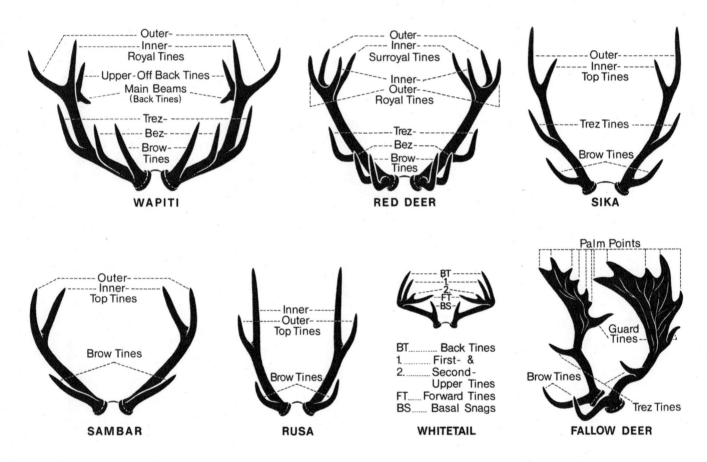

REFERENCES AND SELECTED READING

ANDERSON, J. A., HENDERSON, J. B., *Himalayan Thar in New Zealand. Aspects of Life History and Assessment of Management Problems.* Spec. Publ. No. 2 New Zealand Deerstalkers' Assn, Wellington. 1961. 37 pp. Illus.

BANWELL, D. BRUCE, *Wapiti in New Zealand: The Story of the Fiordland Herd.* A. H. and A. W. Reed, Wellington, 1966. 183 pp. Illus. and maps.

CAHALANE, V. H., "Deer of the World." *National Geographic Magazine*, Vol. LXXVI, No. 4, 463-510. 1939. Illus.

COUTURIER, M. A. J., *Le Chamois: Rupicapra rupicapra* (L). Preface Marcellin de Boule. B. Arthaud, Grenoble, 1938. 855 pp.

DARLING, F. FRASER, *A Herd of Red Deer; A Study in Animal Behaviour.* Oxford University Press, London, 1956. 215pp. Illus. and maps.

DONNE, T. E., *Red Deer Stalking in New Zealand.* Constable and Co., London, 1924. 270pp. Illus. and map.

DONNE, T. E., *The Game Animals of New Zealand: An Account of their Introduction, Acclimatisation, and Development.* John Murray, London, 1924. 322pp. Illus. and map.

HARRIS, L. H., *Hunting Fallow Deer.* New Zealand Forest Service, Wellington, 1967. 16pp. Illus. and maps.

HARRIS, L. H., *Hunting Himalayan Thar.* New Zealand Forest Service, Wellington, 1965. 7pp. Illus. and map.

HARRIS, L. H., *Hunting Red Deer.* New Zealand Forest Service, Wellington, 1967. 18pp. Illus. and maps.

HARRIS, L. H., *Hunting Sambar Deer.* New Zealand Forest Service, Wellington, 1966. 14pp. Illus. and maps.

HARRIS, L. H., *Hunting Sika Deer.* New Zealand Forest Service, Wellington, 1967. 11pp. Illus. and map.

HARRIS, L. H., *Hunting Whitetail Deer.* New Zealand Forest Service, Wellington. 1970. 19 pp. Illus. and maps.

HOWARD, WALTER E., *Control of Introduced Mammals in New Zealand.* Information Series No. 45, Dept. of Scientific and Industrial Research, Wellington. 1965. 96pp. Illus. and maps.

KIDDIE, D. G., *The Sika Deer (Cervus nippon) in New Zealand.* New Zealand Forest Service, Wellington, 1962. 35pp. Illus. and maps.

KLETTE, C., *Notes on Chamois in New Zealand.* Blundell Bros. Ltd., Wellington, 1911. 24pp.

LOGAN, P. C. and HARRIS, L. H., *Introduction and Establishment of Red Deer in New Zealand.* New Zealand Forest Service, Wellington, 1967. 36p. Illus. and maps.

LYDEKKER, RICHARD, *Deer of All Lands. A History of the Family Cervidae Living and Extinct*. London, Rowland Ward Ltd., 1898. 329 pp. Illus.

LYDEKKER, RICHARD, *The Great and Small Game of Europe, Western and Northern Asia and America*. London, Rowland Ward Ltd., 1901. 445 pp.

PHILLIPS-WOLLEY, CLIVE. *Big Game Shooting*. Longmans, Green and Co., London. Second edition 1901. "The Chamois", by W. A. Baillie-Grohman, pp.77-111.

POOLE, A. L., *The New Zealand-American Fiordland Expedition*. Bulletin 103, Dept. of Scientific and Industrial Research, Wellington. 1951. 99pp. Illus. and map.

PRACY, L. T., *Introduction and Liberation of the Opossum (Trichosurus vulpecula) into New Zealand*. New Zealand Forest Service, Wellington, 1962. 28 pp. Map.

RINEY, THANE, *Identification of Big Game Animals in New Zealand*. Dominion Museum, Wellington, 1955. 26pp. Illus.

ROBERTS, GORDON, *Game Animals in New Zealand*. A. H. and A. W. Reed, Wellington, 1968. 112pp. Illus.

THOMSON, GEO. M., *The Naturalisation of Animals and Plants in New Zealand*. Cambridge University Press. London, 1922. 607pp. Illus. and maps.

THOMSON, GEO. M., *Wild Life in New Zealand. Part 1 — Mammalia*. Government Printer, Wellington, 1921. 112pp. Illus.

WODZICKI, K. A., "Ecology and Management of Introduced Ungulates in New Zealand." *La Terre et la Vie,* No. 1, 1961, pp.130-157.

WODZICKI, K. A., *Introduced Mammals of New Zealand: An Ecological and Economic Survey*. Department of Scientific and Industrial Research, Wellington. 1950. 255pp. Illus. and maps.

WODZICKI, K. A., and FLUX, J. E. C., "Guide to Introduced Wallabies in New Zealand". *Tuatara*, vol. 15, No. 2, 1967, pp.47-59.

INDEX

ACKNOWLEDGMENTS

The New Zealand Forest Service acknowledges the advice and assistance given the photographer in the field by many people, especially: Mr M. Curl, Lees Valley; Mr R. L. Edgar, Silverstream; Mr M. Giles, Rahana Station, Maroa; Mr T. R. Giles, Wellington; Mr W. H. Hall, University of Otago; Mr J. A. Hedges, Taupo; Mr A. Hill, Omarama; the Isley family, Galatea; the Jamieson family, Galatea; Mr J. H. McKenzie, Leithen Downs, Waikaka; the Miller family, Paradise; the Mills family, Galatea; Mr J. E. Nutt, Te Awamutu; Mr R. Sewhoy, Frankton; the Shailer family, Rongotea; Mr A. R. Sutherland, Waitahuna; Mr R. S. Veale, Feilding; Mr C. L. Veint, Arcadia Station, Paradise; Mr G. Willis, Te Awamutu; the New Zealand Army; and staff of the Forest Service.